Counterpoint

A Species Approach Based on Schenker's *Counterpoint*

Henry Martin

The Scarecrow Press, Inc.
Lanham, Maryland • Toronto • Oxford
2005

SCARECROW PRESS, INC.

Published in the United States of America
by Scarecrow Press, Inc.
A wholly owned subsidary of
The Rowman & Littlefield Publishing Group, Inc.
4501 Forbes Boulevard, Suite 200, Lanham, Maryland 20706
www.scarecrowpress.com

PO Box 317
Oxford
OX2 9RU, UK

British Library Cataloguing in Publication Information Available

Library of Congress Cataloging-in-Publication Data
Martin, Henry, 1950–
 Counterpoint : a species approach based on Schenker's Counterpoint / Henry
Martin.
  p. cm.
 Includes bibliographical references (p.   ) and index.
 ISBN 0-8108-5409-0 (pbk. : alk. paper)
 1. Counterpoint–Textbooks. I. Schenker, Heinrich, 1868–1935. Kontrapunkt.
English. II. Title.
MT55.M36 2005
781.2'86–dc22   2004018385

™
© The paper used in this publication meets the minimum requirements of
American National Standard for Information Sciences—Permanence of
Paper for Printed Library Materials, ANSI/NISO Z39.48-1992.
Manufactured in the United States of America.

For Pedro —
wonderful musician,
excellent contrapuntalist,
and dear friend

The web site for this book with sample exercises
correlated to each chapter resides at:

http://www.scarecrowpress.com/scp/books/counterpoint/

Contents

Contents

Preface

To the Student

We call music with two or more independent melodic lines *polyphonic* or *contrapuntal*. Such melodies are in *counterpoint*. *Species counterpoint* provides a step-by-step method for learning to combine independent melodies according to idealized norms of sixteenth-century Western European vocal composition. Because of the underlying significance of these norms for tonal music, sixteenth-century principles are applicable to many Western musical genres, including much of the music of our own time.

"Species" is Latin for "type" or "kind." Both "counterpoint" and "contrapuntal" are derived from the Latin "punctus contra punctum," meaning "note against note." The species method of instruction, pioneered in the sixteenth century by such theorists as Giovanni Lanfranco, Vincenzo Lusitano, and Gioseffo Zarlino, was perfected by Johann Joseph Fux (1660–1741), a prominent Austrian composer and theorist, and presented in his famous work *Gradus ad Parnassum* (1725). In learning counterpoint according to Fux's method, musicians progress through gradations of contrapuntal situations that gradually become more complex, i.e., more like "real music" or *free composition*.

Species exercises are just that—exercises—and must not be confused with music. They present common musical situations in simplified settings. Working within the guidelines laid out for each species teaches techniques that refine compositional skills

vii

and bolster musicianship. This procedure is akin to mastering standard scales and arpeggios on a musical instrument in order to perform more effectively. That is, writing species counterpoint is something like practicing "scales for composition." Although the exercises are not actual music, learning to do them well advances compositional technique, just as practicing scales advances instrumental technique.

Let us explore this idea in more detail. Performers find that the major scales are among the first exercises practiced when learning to play an instrument. Why? To begin with, Western melodic instruments are so constructed that the major scales fit them well, and this is because most Western music is based on the major scales or their derivatives. Hence, practicing major scales helps impart the techniques necessary for performing an instrument while teaching the principles underlying the music itself.

A similar kind of relationship applies to species counterpoint and modern composition. Sixteenth-century style is an important antecedent to contemporary Western music. Practicing idealized forms of this earlier style imparts the fundamentals for much modern practice. Moreover, working in an older style sensitizes us to those effects that make contemporary music actually sound contemporary. The subtle differences among musical intervals and their contrapuntal and harmonic implications resonate more deeply. A study of species counterpoint also enhances voice-leading fluency (how notes connect to other notes) and cannot help but enrich any contemporary practice and understanding, whatever its stylistic basis.

One of my favorite composers, Johannes Brahms, often began his day with counterpoint, as a way of "warming up" to composition, just as a performer might warm up with scales or exercises. Sometimes, Brahms's practice with counterpoint would generate a musical idea that he could later use when he took up his real work. Approaching the study of counterpoint in this spirit will maximize its value.

Prerequisite Theory and Keyboard Skills

• key signatures

• major and minor scales

• whole, half, quarter, eighth, and sixteenth notes with their associated rests and the ability to count them in the standard time signatures: 2/2 ("cut time"), 3/2, 4/4, and 3/4

• intervals (reviewed below)

• the treble (G) and bass (F) clefs (alto and tenor clefs to be learned while studying the species)

• the basics of functional harmony (recommended, but not essential, in studying two-part writing; even more helpful in three-part writing)

• sight-singing of simple melodies

• playing a keyboard with "easy piano" fluency

How to Practice Species Counterpoint

In studying any music theory, it is important to hear as well as understand any item being taught. This is particularly true with species counterpoint. Because of its simplicity, it is possible to write species exercises mechanically. Such an approach, however, will not encourage musical growth as much as actually working with both the mind and the ear.

A student of mine once claimed that studying species excercises was useless because, as he put it, "I can write a computer program to do this perfectly." I tried to show him that being able to write such a program was irrelevant. For example, just because musicians can program synthesizers to perform scales rapidly and cleanly does not mean that they can play the scales themselves on a keyboard. The act of doing the work while internalizing, listening to, and comparing results is important.

Rather than approach species exercises mechanically, I recommend this procedure:

• Try to write some species counterpoint every day, perhaps as a warm-up before practicing or composing, or as a break from either.

• Sing the cantus firmus. If necessary, play it on the piano or another instrument repeatedly to be sure it is fully internalized, i.e., that you can hear it in your mind. If singing the cantus firmus is difficult, spend time working on singing samples of cantus firmi every day before writing.

• Do the exercise on paper away from the piano. While completing the exercise, try to hear it mentally.

• Pay attention to correct notation. Writing species exercises provides an opportunity to learn to notate music correctly, a skill that will repay itself many times over in professional situations. Consider notating your examples with a computer program and compare your handwritten results to the computer's.

• After completing the exercise mentally, sing the cantus firmus again, then sing the added counterpoint. If singing the added line is difficult, the line itself may be awkward and should be improved.

• When the exercise is complete, examine it visually. Is its shape satisfying? Visual examination of notation is often musically insightful: if the music looks awkward, it may sound awkward. Visual examination may suggest ideas for further revision.

• When the exercise is complete, has no mistakes, and is visually satisfying, play it at the piano. In addition to help with ear training, species exercises provide an opportunity for improving keyboard and sight-reading skills.

• It is surprising that exercises often do not sound the same "live" as first heard mentally or when the lines are sung separately. An important goal in working through species exercises is to match more closely the mental sound image of an exercise and its eventual keyboard realization.

• Evaluate the fluency of the exercise on the keyboard. Make improvements while trying not to introduce any mistakes.

• When the exercise satisfies you musically, try this additional ear-training exercise: play one part on the piano while singing the other.

• Advanced students may wish to transpose the exercises to other keys, particularly if they lie outside comfortable vocal ranges.

• Return to the same exercise the next day and play it again. It is often surprising to discover that although the exercise sounded fine earlier, it is no longer satisfying. Continue to improve the exercise, a procedure that helps in learning to revise real music.

• When the exercise seems to offer no further opportunities for improvement, proceed to another example. After completing a new example, return to the first exercise. Again, it is often surprising to find that it no longer sounds as compelling as it did previously.

• For each cantus firmus assigned, do at least two examples, one below and one above the cantus firmus. Schoenberg recommends putting a cantus firmus in the middle of a page of music paper and filling the entire page with possible counterpoint lines above and below.

Please note the page references to Schenker (1910, 1922) at the beginning of most chapters. Although Schenker's monumental study forms the basis of this text, it is not necessary to refer to it unless you wish to study some topic in detail. Of the other studies listed in the bibliography, Fux (1725)—the basis of the species method itself—is inexpensive and widely available. For applications of this method to musical analysis, I especially recommend Salzer–Schachter (1969). Schoenberg (1963) is excellent and systematically reviews many of the ideas found below with numerous musical examples. A more informal approach than a strict species model, it develops free composition as well.

To the Instructor

This volume attempts to distill Schenker's contrapuntal insights, as detailed in the insightful and masterly *Counterpoint* (1910, 1922), into a reference manual for practice in composition and musicianship. It can either supplement other theory work or function as a stand-alone text. Musical examples will be made available on this book's web site; however, I do recommend that the instructor supply original musical examples for the students to copy during class. In my experience, when students copy material from the board, they study it in more detail than when it is readily available on the page and often glanced at quickly.

One of Schenker's most important legacies was his reconsideration of the purpose of species counterpoint. Whereas his predecessors equated study of the species with composition itself, Schenker's view was that species counterpoint provided a neat idealization of the compositional process as well as profound insight into tonal musical coherence. Further, Schenker insisted that species counterpoint must not be confused with free composition, where its abstractions were constantly being overridden, particularly at the foreground.

Schenker published his results in two volumes far too extensive for use as classroom texts, but they are important sources for anyone hoping to maximize the value of a counterpoint class. Schenker's view of counterpoint laid the groundwork for his analytical method, which took form during the 1920s and eventually culminated in *Der freie Satz* (1935). After Schenker's death in 1935, his students continued to stress the importance of counterpoint in Schenkerian-based analysis with many important studies, including Salzer–Schachter's *Counterpoint in Composition* (1969).

It is evident that this volume duplicates neither Schenker's completeness nor his subtlety in dealing with the many possibilities of interacting lines. In the treatment of the combined species especially, where explanations can become quite complex, the text functions as a general outline. For convenience, the page numbers in each chapter are correlated with Schenker's original study.

Aside from Schenker's involved explanations of the combined species, it is ironic that as the number of voices—and thereby the complexity of the music—increases, Schenker has less and less to say. A cynic might claim that Schenker was running out of steam, but a more likely explanation is that counterpoint is essentially melodic; it is clearest and best analyzed with two to three parts. Hence, Schenker's commentary is more extensive whenever the voices are unencumbered by complex texture, which can overwhelm melodic clarity. Indeed, he discusses the cantus firmus for some ninety-two pages!

Rather than restate Schenker's observations solely as rules, I have sometimes added brief musical justifications. Often these considerations are Schenker's own, but from time to time his discussion of a certain principle might be very opaque, if not obscure. In such instances, I might state that "it's been done this way traditionally," rather than paraphrase Schenker's reasoning. One such example is the explanation of why suspensions must resolve downward. His justifications seem to me unpersuasive, so I think it best to inform students that for the purposes of species, it is easier to get control over the technique by restricting resolutions downward. Further, this direction is both more common and more natural for relaxing tension.

The rules for each species type are divided into "Absolutes" and "Preferences and Hints." Classroom experience has shown that such a division clarifies instruction by contrasting what is absolutely wrong (say, a parallel fifth) to what may or may not be musically acceptable under given circumstances. Over time, it usually becomes clear to the students why the "absolute" rules are absolute: when they are broken, the musical outcome is rarely positive (certainly within the stylistic microcosm of species counterpoint). The "preference" rules are more arbitrary and may depend on circumstances or aesthetic taste. As the species model grows more complex, the student's task begins to resemble free composition where relatively few absolute rules apply.

It has been my experience that certain absolute rules, such as the dissonance of the perfect fourth harmonically (in two-part writing), are first questioned by students as incorrect, incomprehensible, or at least highly dependent on musical circumstances. Early on, therefore, I make a point of playing two-part examples in class in which the fourth is incorrectly treated as a consonance. By so doing, it quickly becomes clear why this prohibition is ranked as "absolute."

It is also helpful for the students to understand that the species model is a laboratory, a controlled environment in which musical processes, both simplified and slowed down, can be examined under a microscope. It is a way of learning techniques in a radically restricted context so that the musical effect of each introduced item is focused on, tested, and then practiced. The second species, for example, introduces the concept of harmonic dissonance and determines how it should be treated. The third species is especially helpful for the development of melodic flow. It can be argued that the second species is the most difficult and important of the five settings. Whereas the additional notes provided by the third species allow one to work out of tight corners, problems in the second species (and in combinations that include it) sometimes entail rewriting much of the exercise.

By working in the laboratory of the species method, students become aware of the pluses and minuses of compositional decisions. In their own music they may decide to break given species rules, but—having studied them—they will do so more intelligently, with more understanding of the effect, both technically and emotionally. For example, I might say, "For our purposes, the tritone is a melodic dissonance. You may not use it in a species melody. In your own music, you may use it freely, but you will hear it more fully; you will appreciate its special status rather than taking it for granted."

Class discussion should focus on the fluency of the students' exercises. In addition to citing the merits or demerits of their work (anonymously if possible), I find it helpful to adduce excerpts from actual compositions that exemplify the techniques of the species exercises. Fine examples can be found in the original Schenker as well as in Salzer–Schachter (1969). Excerpts from the contemporary repertory, including jazz and popular music, are also effective.

I tend to favor the minor mode over the major in the cantus firmi assigned as exercises (which may be modified by the instructor). This is because the two forms of the melodic minor are more difficult for students to handle than the single-form major. Further, writing with the descending melodic minor amounts to using the relative major implicitly; in the course of the exercise, raising the lowered $\hat{6}$ and $\hat{7}$ creates a modulation from the relative major to the tonic minor. Writing in the minor mode thus accustoms students to issues in modulation more generally, particularly cross relations. This topic, introduced in chapter 1, is taken up in chapter 16.

Since the major-minor system has become the basis of common-practice tonality, I agree with Schenker in discouraging exercises in the other diatonic modes. These seem too specialized for students approaching counterpoint as a tool for improving compositional skills and overall musicianship.

I usually assign the well-known Fux D minor cantus firmus as the first exercise to be set after the presentation of new material, largely because of the elegant simplicity of the cantus. Not containing $\hat{6}$ and $\hat{7}$, the Fux D minor presents fewer problems than other minor-mode cantus firmi. As a result, students can write in F major through most of the setting, only raising $\hat{6}$ and $\hat{7}$ for the cadence. In subsequent exercises, the minor-mode cantus firmi that are assigned usually have a raised $\hat{6}$ and $\hat{7}$. These are more difficult (especially in three parts) because of potential cross relations and leading-tone doublings.

* * *

After years of teaching species counterpoint according to the method presented here, I have developed procedures and schedules that work effectively. For a semester of fourteen or fifteen weeks, a beginning class meeting one hour a week can treat two-part species quite thoroughly. One exercise is assigned as homework each week.

The second semester, also with fourteen or fifteen classes meeting one hour a week, focuses on three-part writing. Whereas Schenker originally presented all five three-part simple species before examining the combined species, I have found it preferable to include combined examples earlier on. It enlivens the class and more quickly introduces the students to real-world musical situations likely to arise in their other work.

For a third semester, I finish any remaining chapters in three-part species writing, then introduce material that leads to basic two-part free composition in this idealized renaissance style. This goes beyond Schenker's original study but is included here for those instructors who would like to continue the basic approach. This third semester can also serve as an introduction to the study of baroque style.

There are three main problems encountered by students of renaissance free composition: 1) writing without cantus firmus, 2) writing points of imitation, and 3) modulating to other key centers for the purposes of interior cadences. In addition to addressing these issues, the other techniques to be taught are inversion, augmentation and diminution, and invertible counterpoint. I have found that in a second-year (third-semester) class meeting one hour per week for fourteen or fifteen sessions, it is possible for most motivated students to produce a short two-part composition in this idealized renaissance style.

Finally, appendices are included of material which the instructor may assign as supplementary or the students may use for self-study. These appendices may be especially useful for a class meeting more than one hour a week, in which time is available to pursue four-part species and a study of three-part free composition.

Acknowledgments

My principal debt is to Schenker's *Counterpoint* (1910, 1922), which underlies the material in Parts One and Two and the species sections of Part Three.

The material in Part Three was in part influenced by *Polyphonic Composition* (Swindale 1962). This text formed the basis of a superb renaissance composition class at the University of Michigan in the 1970s taught by Ellwood Derr. I was fortunate to be a member of his class.

Schoenberg's *Preliminary Exercises in Counterpoint* (1963) has been very helpful in extending the species material to free composition. I also use Schoenberg's concept of *neutralization* of the variable $\hat{6}$ and $\hat{7}$ scale degrees in the minor mode.

I am not sure where I picked up the idea of labeling intervals with triangles and circles; it was perhaps from a student who used this procedure elsewhere. In any event, I would like to thank whoever invented this technique.

I would especially like to thank my counterpoint students. From 1990 to 1998, I taught species counterpoint at the New School Jazz Program (New School University, New York City), where this text gradually took shape. My students helped improve earlier versions of the manuscript. Among them, I must especially acknowledge John Ellis, Arun Luthra, Pedro Moreira, and Emanuel Rueffler, who caught several errors and provided many excellent suggestions. This book is dedicated to Pedro.

Terms and Notation

The *cantus firmus* is the given whole-note melody that forms the basis of the exercise. "Cantus firmus" in this volume is abbreviated "CF."

The *contrapuntal* melodies (the *counterpoints*) are written against the cantus firmus. "Counterpoint" in this volume is usually abbreviated "ctpt."

"Voice," "part," and "line" are synonymous and refer to the contrapuntal melodies. One such "voice" or "part" would be the cantus firmus.

An *interval* is the distance between two notes. A *compound interval* is the "same" interval extended beyond an octave. For example, a ninth is the compound interval of a second and would thus take on the same names (minor, major, etc.) as a second. To name an interval, construct the major scale from the lower note:

a) When the upper note coincides with the major-scale note, then:
- the interval is "perfect" when it is a unison or prime (1), fourth (4), fifth (5), or octave (8) (and their compound intervals)
- the interval is "major" when it is a second (2), third (3), sixth (6), or seventh (7) (and their compound intervals)

b) When the upper note is a half step flatter (or lower) than the major-scale note, then:
- the interval is "diminished" when it a unison, fourth, fifth, or octave (and their compound intervals)
- the interval is "minor" when it is a second, third, sixth, or seventh (and their compound intervals)

c) When the upper note is a half step sharper (or higher) than the major-scale note, then the interval is "augmented" for all interval types.

d) When the upper note is two half steps flatter (or lower) than the major-scale note, then:
- the interval is "double diminished" when it is a unison, fourth, fifth, or octave (and their compound intervals)
- the interval is "diminished" when it is a second, third, sixth, or seventh (and their compound intervals)

e) When the upper note is two half steps sharper (or higher) than the major-scale note, then the interval is "double augmented" for all interval types.

Intervals reckoned from a given bass note are referred to as 1 for unison, 2 for second, 5 for fifth, etc. These are assumed to be major-scale intervals for major-mode keys and minor-scale intervals for minor-mode keys unless prefixed by ♭ (flat) or ♯ (sharp).

Scale steps or *degrees* within a key are also referred to by Arabic numerals with a caret (^). Hence, in the key of F, A is $\hat{3}$, the third scale degree. In F minor, A♭ is $\hat{3}$, although to emphasize its flatness relative to the major mode, it may sometimes be called ♭$\hat{3}$. When referring to the sixth and seventh scale degrees in minor, I use ↓$\hat{6}$ and ↓$\hat{7}$ to refer to the lowered versions and ↑$\hat{6}$ and ↑$\hat{7}$ for the raised versions.

When register is irrelevant, pitches are referred to simply as C, C♯, etc. When register needs to be clarified, numerals are appended to the note to refer to a specific octave spanning C up to B: middle C = C4, the C an octave above middle C = C5, the C an octave below middle C = C3, etc. A♭ a major tenth below middle C is, for example, A♭2; E a major tenth above middle C is E5.

Web Site Information

The web site for this text has sample exercises correlated to each chapter. Step-by-step suggestions accompany each exercise. The web site resides at:

http://www.scarecrowpress.com/scp/books/counterpoint/

From the home page of the web site, you may proceed directly to the exercises for each chapter or the appendices.

Part One

Two-Part Counterpoint

Chapter 1

Exercise Writing and the Cantus Firmus

[Schenker 1, 17–109]

Cantus firmus (CF) is Latin for "fixed melody." Its plural is *cantus firmi.* Using only whole notes, CFs are the basic melodies against which various lines are written in *counterpoint* (ctpt.). As described in the preface, each line of counterpoint explores a different rhythmic *species* while the CF maintains the basic rhythm of one whole note per bar.

This chapter is introductory in that it does not discuss counterpoint per se. Instead, it treats melodic lines in general, so as to delineate the basic principles of the idealized renaissance practice that underlies the study of species counterpoint. We will describe the general melodic lines in this chapter as if they were cantus firmi, although most of the principles are applicable to any contrapuntal lines that arise through the species methods.

The rules below are extensive. Although they should be studied closely, they need not be thoroughly mastered before proceeding to chapter 2. Progressing through the text and completing the assignments will provide considerable practice in writing the kinds of melodies described here.

3

Absolute Rules

The Exercise as a Whole

1. Write in "cut time" (2/2) with each exercise 10–16 bars long. (Later, exercises in 3/2 should be tried as well; most modifications to the rules will be clear.)

2. Write each part with a specific vocal range in mind: soprano (C4–G5), alto (G3–D5), tenor (C3–G4), and bass (F2–C4). These ranges may be relaxed in lines conceived more instrumentally. For example, a bassline to be played on the piano may go lower than F2.

3. Use only the major mode and melodic minor mode (i.e., the traditional melodic minor with ↓6̂ and ↓7̂ descending and ↑6̂ and ↑7̂ ascending).

The Cantus Firmus

4. Write whole notes; one per bar.

5. Begin and end on the same tonic note.

6. There is typically only one cadence in a species exercise, occurring at the end. Descending cadences for the CF: 3̂-2̂-1̂; 1̂-2̂-1̂; 4̂-2̂-1̂.

7. For the purposes of single-line practice in CF writing, ascending cadences may be used. (In contrapuntal exercises, I provide only CFs with descending cadences.) Ascending cadences: ↑6̂-↑7̂-1̂; 1̂-↑7̂-1̂; 5̂-↑7̂-1̂; 2̂-↑7̂-1̂.

All Species Melodies (Including the CF)

8. Keep all melodies within the range of a tenth, which will make them easier to sing.

9. Do not immediately repeat a note, as this interrupts melodic flow. (Exception: notes may be repeated in melodies written in the first species, as discussed in the next chapter.)

10. Avoid chromatic pitches. (In the major mode, that is. Some chromatic alterations to pitches are necessary in the melodic minor, as noted in the next rule. In addition, two other common exceptions are noted below in rule #20.)

11. Use the ascending and descending forms of the melodic minor correctly:

a) In an ascending melody, $\uparrow\hat{6}$ must at some point proceed to $\uparrow\hat{7}$ and to $\hat{1}$ before any use of $\downarrow\hat{6}$ and $\downarrow\hat{7}$.

b) In a descending melody, $\downarrow\hat{7}$ must proceed at some point to $\downarrow\hat{6}$ and then to $\hat{5}$ before any use of $\uparrow\hat{6}$ and $\uparrow\hat{7}$.

These resolutions to $\hat{1}$ or $\hat{5}$ respectively *neutralize* the tendencies of the unstable $\hat{6}$ and $\hat{7}$ in the melodic minor. Once the lowered versions are neutralized to $\hat{5}$, melodies can ascend through the raised versions; once the raised versions are neutralized to $\hat{1}$, melodies can descend through the lowered versions. There is a strong sense in which the descending melodic minor mode implies the relative major key. Hence, before the exercise is completed, try to *cancel* the $\downarrow\hat{6}$ and $\downarrow\hat{7}$ by returning to $\uparrow\hat{6}$ and $\uparrow\hat{7}$, and then to $\hat{1}$. In canceling the $\downarrow\hat{6}$ and $\downarrow\hat{7}$, the minor tonic key area will be regained before the final cadence.

12. Avoid all dissonant intervals of the major and minor modes in melodic writing. In particular:

a) no tritones (e.g., $\hat{4}$-$\hat{7}$ in major, or $\hat{4}$-$\uparrow\hat{7}$ and $\hat{2}$-$\downarrow\hat{6}$ in minor)
b) no sevenths of any kind

13. Avoid all chromatic intervals found in the minor mode (or produced by unresolved combinations of ascending and descending minor-mode forms):

a) no $\uparrow\hat{7}$ and $\hat{3}$ (dim. 4th or aug. 5th)
b) no $\uparrow\hat{7}$ and $\downarrow\hat{6}$ (aug. 2nd or dim. 7th)
c) no $\downarrow\hat{6}$ and $\uparrow\hat{6}$ (aug. unison)
d) no $\downarrow\hat{7}$ and $\uparrow\hat{7}$ (aug. unison)

14. Avoid outlining dissonant intervals, e.g., a D4-F4-C5 (dissonant seventh from D4-C5) or F4-G4-B4 (dissonant tritone from F4-B4).

15. Avoid melodic patterns, e.g., C-E-D-F-E-G-F-A.

16. Avoid consecutive large intervals, e.g., F4-F5-C5.

17. Avoid leaps of more than an octave.

18. Avoid more than three leaps in a row (although an occasional triadic arpeggiation may be permissible). Avoid more than four melodic successions, by either step or skip, in the same direction. (In a difficult passage, you may use five successions in the same direction.)

19. Avoid outlining seventh chords, e.g., C4-E4-G4-B4.

20. Exceptions to the avoidance of chromaticism include the following neighbor motions, which are permissible:

a) $\hat{6}$-$\flat\hat{7}$-$\hat{6}$ (major mode only)
b) $\hat{5}$-$\sharp\hat{4}$-$\hat{5}$ (both major and minor modes)

The use of $\flat\hat{7}$ and $\sharp\hat{4}$ neighbor tones imply brief modulations to (or *tonicizations* of) the IV and V tonal areas respectively. As noted in later chapters, dissonant neighbors are prohibited in second and third species lines, hence any use of these neighbors must be consonant. When the ♭$\hat{7}$ proceeds to $\hat{6}$ or the ♯$\hat{4}$ proceeds to $\hat{5}$, the chromatic pitch has been *resolved* and its non-chromatic form may be used. Any chromatic pitch must be resolved before its non-chromatic form can be used.

21. Any use of a chromatic pitch must be *canceled* by its diatonic form within the same octave before the end of exercise. For example, after using the chromatic pitches ♭$\hat{7}$ and ♯$\hat{4}$ (as in the preceding rule) and properly resolving them, they must be canceled. Cancellation of the chromatic pitch signals return to the tonic key. (In the case of rule #11 above, the neutralization of ↓$\hat{6}$ and ↓$\hat{7}$ indicates potential return of the ascending minor mode with ↑$\hat{6}$ and ↑$\hat{7}$, thus canceling ↓$\hat{6}$ and ↓$\hat{7}$.)

22. Avoid *cross relations*, i.e., chromatic, unresolved versions of the same note appearing in different octaves. For example, in the key of C major do not write a B3 in one voice after a B♭4 in another voice until the B♭4 has first been resolved to A4.

Preference Rules and Hints: All Species Melodies (Including the CF)

23. Emphasize seconds as the basic unit of melodic construction. Your melodies should feature seconds more than any other particular interval.

24. Build the exercise to a high point, then descend to the cadence.

25. After a leap of a fourth, fifth, or octave, try to return by step in the opposite direction. Successive leaps of a third in the same direction are occasionally permissible if not overused. (See rule #18 above.)

26. Leaps of a sixth are rare in sixteenth-century style. They should generally be avoided, except, perhaps, for the minor sixth upwards, which is the easiest to sing.

27. Avoid monotony, which often results from repeating notes excessively within a restricted range; that is, the same note or group of notes returns too often. Monotonous melodies lack direction.

28. Always sing any melody that you have written. If it is difficult to sing, it may have too many leaps, both dissonant and consonant. Eliminate dissonant leaps entirely; generally restrict consonant leaps of a fourth or greater to two or three per exercise. Use leaps of a third freely, but do not allow them to dominate stepwise motion.

Exercise

Exercise 1-1: Write ten cantus firmi, five in the major mode, five in the minor. Use a different key for each CF. Use a variety of clefs and a variety of vocal ranges (soprano, alto, tenor, and bass). Stay within the proper range for each voice and keep each melody within the range of a tenth.

Chapter 2

Two-Part First Species
(Note Against Note)

[Schenker 1, 110–75]

The first species (note against note) consists of a whole note in the ctpt. sounding against a whole note in the CF.

The first species presents entirely consonant relationships between the ctpt. and the CF, thus providing an excellent opportunity to solidify recognizing and writing the consonant intervals. The sole use of whole notes in each line provides the simplest possible environment to study the behavior of two lines in counterpoint. The lack of rhythmic interaction between the lines makes it easier to focus on the individual effects of the consonant intervals and the overall shapes of the melodies. Because it is also the easiest to play on the piano, the first species is a good place to begin working on increasing keyboard fluency.

Rhythmic differentiation and various kinds of dissonances will be introduced in subsequent species. The concepts introduced in this chapter carry over to these more complicated interactions.

In two-part writing, we call each part "treble" or "bass" (or "upper" and "lower") with one of them the CF, the other the added ctpt. When the CF is below, the species line is called the *upper counterpoint*; with the CF above, the species line is called

9

the *lower counterpoint.* Generally in two-part writing, the voices should remain in the same registral disposition to each other; that is, they should not cross. (In multi-voice settings, the parts are allowed to cross occasionally.)

In two-part writing, it is customary to use voices that are next to one another registrally. Hence, write for soprano and alto, alto and tenor, or tenor and bass. While you can use G (treble) clef and F (bass) clef for all parts, it is recommended that you use alto clef for the alto voice and tenor clef for the tenor voice.

Absolutes

1. For each assigned cantus firmus, write at least two exercises: one with the ctpt. below the CF, the other with the ctpt. above the CF. Choose voice pairings that are next to one another (soprano-alto, alto-tenor, or tenor-bass). Strive for correct notation by aligning the whole notes.

2. Follow the principles of melodic writing set forth in chapter 1 on the cantus firmus and melody in general. *Review*: no dissonant melodic intervals; no chordal outlining; no patterns; no consecutive large skips; follow any large skips with stepwise motion in the opposite direction; generally no chromaticism (except with $\hat{6}$ and $\hat{7}$ in minor); stay within the range of a tenth; keep the melody simple and flowing.

3. Begin the exercise with a perfect consonant interval. These, in descending order of perfection (relative to the overtone series), are the unison or prime, octave, and perfect fifth (1, 8, and 5). In the upper ctpt., either of these are permissible. In the lower ctpt., you may use only an octave or unison (8 or 1), since the perfect fifth below the tonic of the CF is the subdominant pitch, which implies starting in the (incorrect) key of the subdominant. You must avoid the lower fifth at the beginning of *all* two-part exercises.

4. Only harmonic consonances may be written between the CF and the ctpt. in the main body of the exercise. They are:

a) the *perfect* consonant intervals (see rule #3)

b) the *imperfect* consonant intervals, which in descending order of perfection (relative to the overtone series) are the major third, minor third, minor sixth, and major sixth (3 and 6)

c) the extensions of the perfect and imperfect consonant intervals beyond the octave as *compound intervals*

5. Another way of stating rule #4 is that no harmonic dissonances may be used in first species. The harmonic dissonances to be avoided are:

a) the perfect fourth (although this interval is a *melodic* consonance and hence may be used freely *within* any melody)

b) all seconds and sevenths

c) all tritones (including 4̂-7̂ in major; and 4̂-↓7̂ and 2̂-↓6̂ in minor)

d) all chromatic intervals

e) all the above extended beyond the octave as compound intervals

6. There are four possible types of two-part melodic motion, which characterize the relationship between any pair of voices:

a) *parallel* (e.g., A4-C5 to G4-B4)
b) *contrary* (e.g., A4-C5 to E5-G4)
c) *similar* (e.g., A4-C5 to B4-G5)
d) *oblique* (e.g., A4-C5 to A4-F5)

For oblique motion, one of the parts must repeat a pitch; this *is* permissible in the first species only (see rule #17 below) but is usually weak.

7. *Parallel motion:*

a) Between imperfect consonances, parallel motion is always permissible and is very common (i.e., parallel thirds and sixths). However, do not use more than three parallel imperfect consonances in a row, because the independence of the parts is compromised.

b) Between perfect consonances, parallel motion must be avoided—thus the most famous rule of counterpoint: no parallel fifths or octaves. In this context, they sound empty and reduce the feeling of independence in each part.

8. *Contrary motion:*

a) Between imperfect consonances, contrary motion is always permissible and emphasizes the independence of the parts.

b) Between imperfect and perfect consonances, contrary motion is always permissible and emphasizes the independence of the parts.

c) Between perfect consonances, contrary motion is permissible if the intervals are different; the musical effect, however, is weak because the consecutive intervals are harmonically empty. Contrary motion between perfect consonances of the same type is called an *anti-parallel* and is prohibited; it also sounds empty.

9. *Similar motion:*

a) Between imperfect consonances, similar motion is always permissible.

b) From an imperfect consonance to a perfect consonance, *similar motion must be avoided.*

c) From a perfect consonance to an imperfect consonance, similar motion is always permissible.

10. *Oblique motion:* oblique motion is permissible between all combinations of perfect and imperfect consonances, but it should be used sparingly because the repeated notes create the effect of a single note held out awkwardly.

11. Avoid connecting major thirds by stepwise motion of a major second. They result in a tritone between the lower pitch of one of the thirds and the upper pitch of the other. (With more parts, such a motion is usually disguised and can be permissible.)

12. Keep the parts within a tenth of each other; you may allow them to be a twelfth apart in a difficult situation.

13. Avoid cross relations between parts (e.g., G4-B4 to Bb4-D5). Note that this is still considered a cross relation, although the B4 and Bb4 are in the same register.

14. Avoid crossing one part over the pitch in the previous bar of the other part (e.g., C4-E4 to F4-D5). This is called an *overlap.*

15. The only possible cadences in first species:

a) sixth to octave for the upper ctpt.
b) third to unison in the lower ctpt. (or tenth to octave)

Hence the exercise ends with a perfect octave or unison preceded by $\hat{2}$-$\uparrow\hat{7}$ in the second-to-last ("penultimate") measure. The $\hat{2}$ will always be in the CF, so the ctpt. must reach $\uparrow\hat{7}$ by the penultimate bar. In the minor mode, the $\downarrow\hat{7}$ must be raised to create the leading tone. When the $\uparrow\hat{7}$ is preceded by $\downarrow\hat{6}$, the $\downarrow\hat{6}$ must also be raised to $\uparrow\hat{6}$, thus effecting the melodic minor scale. The combination of $\hat{2}$ and $\uparrow\hat{7}$ in the penultimate bar implies a dominant harmony resolving to a tonic harmony at the octave or unison of the last bar.

Preferences and Hints

16. In the main body of the piece, emphasize imperfect consonances. These will contrast the perfect consonances beginning and ending the exercise and give the exercise a feeling of forward motion.

17. Keep the added counterpoint flowing—yet if necessary a tone may be repeated. Notes may be repeated in first-species melodies only.

18. Try to build the exercise gracefully to a high point, then descend for the cadence.

19. It is often easier to create the exercise backwards from the cadence. That is, after beginning the exercise try to establish the cadence, then complete the material in between. This advice pertains to all species exercises, though every composer will find a preferred way to work. (There will be more on working methods as we proceed.)

20. As outlined in the preface: compose away from the piano and try to hear the exercise mentally. After you think the exercise is correct and musically compelling, sing each line, then play the exercise at the piano and make any changes you can to improve it. Check it again later, preferably on another day.

21. Species counterpoint provides an excellent opportunity to learn alto and tenor clefs. These are important if you plan to work with string instruments or orchestral music. Viola parts, for example, are normally read in alto clef, where the middle line of the staff is middle C. It is a convenient clef for a midrange melody that requires too many ledger lines in either treble or bass

clef, since it is located exactly between them. Tenor clef, with middle C located on the fourth line, is slightly less common but important nonetheless; it is most often found in parts for bassoons, trombones, cellos, and basses. As stated above, write parts conceived for alto voice in alto clef and parts for tenor voice in tenor clef.

Exercises

For each exercise, write at least two ctpts., one above and one below the CF. Write each part on a separate staff. Be sure the notes between the staves are properly aligned. Write your CF in ink, so that you will not erase it by mistake when working on the ctpt.

For all exercises, label your intervals. For two-part writing, merely write the interval number between staves with each part.

For a perfect consonance, enclose the interval number in a triangle. The triangle will focus your attention on that perfect interval: whenever two triangles in a row occur, it is a weakness and maybe also an error; revise accordingly. For each triangle, check to be sure that the perfect consonance is not approached through similar motion. Be sure that triangles begin and end the exercise. Be sure that there are not more than one or two triangles in the middle of the exercise. Even two may sound excessive.

Although the CFs are given throughout this book with specific pitches in specific keys, they may be transposed to other octaves or keys to create CFs for different voices. For example, the CF in Exercise 2-1 (the Fux D-minor CF) best suits the alto voice. It could be transposed down an octave to create a bass CF. It could be transposed down a fifth (to G minor) to create a CF for the tenor. It could be transposed up a fifth (to A minor) to create a CF for the soprano.

Complete the following exercises in two-part first species. Remember to set at least one upper and lower ctpt. for each CF (Follow this advice for all two-part exercises.)

Exercise 2-1 (The Fux D-minor CF): D4 - F4 - E4 - D4 - G4 - F4 - A4 - G4 - F4 - E4 - D4 (This well-known cantus firmus is the first to appear in Fux's *Gradus ad Parnassum* [Fux 1725].)

Exercise 2-2: B3 - D4 - E4 - F♯4 - G♯4 - A♯4 - B4 - F♯4 - D4 - C♯4 - B3 (in B minor)

Exercise 2-3: G4 - A4 - C5 - B♭4 - E♭5 - D5 - F♯4 - G4 - C5 - B♭4 - A4 - G4 (in G minor)

Chapter 3

Two-Part Second Species (Two Notes Against One)

[Schenker 1, 176–226]

This species consists of two half notes in the ctpt. against the whole note of the CF. In cut time (2/2), the first beat of the bar is called the *downbeat*, the second beat of the bar is the *upbeat*.

Note the rhythmic interaction of the parts: they coincide at the downbeats, which are thereby emphasized relative to the upbeats where single notes sound through the sustained CF note. The repeated emphases on the downbeats from bar to bar set up the 2/2 meter. In the first species, no meter was aurally apparent.

The effect of the 2/2 meter highlights a simple musical truth: we tend to hear as downbeats (as relatively accented, that is) musical moments where, in a slowly repeating rhythmic pattern, parts coincide. It follows that downbeats should be treated in a manner musically different than upbeats: because downbeats are more important structurally, the music should reflect this simple hierarchy. The second species respects this hierarchy by stipulating that downbeats must be consonant, whereas upbeats may be consonant or dissonant.

Species counterpoint is elegantly cumulative. Most of what is new about a particular species carries over into the next and subsequent species. For example, the most important technique studied in the first species is the connection of perfect and imperfect consonances through the four types of motion: parallel, similar, contrary, and oblique. What was learned regarding these types of motion carries over to the second, then to all subsequent species. Similarly, the rules of melodic structure studied in chapter 1 apply to all species melodies.

Absolutes

1. The exercise must begin with a perfect consonance, as in all two-part species exercises. As always, the lower fifth is excluded, because it changes the key.

2. Keep the voices within a tenth (occasionally a twelfth), as in all two-part writing.

3. Do not allow the voices to cross, as in all two-part writing.

4. The ctpt. should generally begin with a half-rest coinciding with the downbeat of the CF. The entrance of the ctpt. on the upbeat must be a perfect consonance.

5. All downbeats must be consonant as in the first species.

6. The upbeats may be consonant or dissonant. (Again, the upbeat at the beginning of the exercise must be a perfect consonance.)

7. A dissonant upbeat must be approached and left by step in the same direction; i.e., a dissonant upbeat must be a *passing tone*. (This is the key rule of the second species.)

8. Dissonant neighboring tones are not allowed. (A *neighboring tone* moves stepwise from a note, then returns to it.) Dissonant neighbors are not allowed because 1) the counterpoint does not take the simplest route, i.e., continue in the same direction (es-

sentially Schenker's justification), and 2) they greatly simplify writing the exercises.

9. Consonant upbeats may be approached and left by skip. By combining first-species concepts with this rule and rule #7, we arrive at what may be the most important general species principle: consonant intervals may be approached and left by skip, whereas dissonant intervals must be treated by stepwise motion. The general principle of stepwise treatment of dissonance versus freer treatment of consonance will admit of some exceptions and refinements, but in general it should be borne in mind as the most important consonance-dissonance rule in the system of species counterpoint.

10. The second species can be broken down into three temporal relationships between the voices: a) upbeat to the following downbeat, b) downbeat to the following downbeat, and c) upbeat to the following upbeat. Each case in turn:

a) Similar and parallel motion from an upbeat to a perfect consonance on the downbeat must be avoided. Thus, the first-species rules continue to apply but are shifted to the latter part of the bar.

b) Parallel perfect consonances from downbeat to downbeat are permissible if the intervening upbeat is a skip larger than a third and the motion from upbeat to downbeat is contrary. Too many of them, however, create a poor effect. Similar motion between perfect consonances from downbeat to downbeat is generally permissible.

c) Parallel and similar motion between perfect consonances is permissible from upbeat to upbeat, but too many in succession create a poor effect.

11. Avoid the *ottava battuta*, which occurs when the lower voice proceeds by step to the octave while the upper (in contrary motion) proceeds by a leap.

12. Notes must not be repeated in the second-species line. (Recall that notes may only be repeated in first-species lines.)

13. There is only one possible cadence in the second species: because the penultimate bar must have $\hat{2}$ in the CF, the ctpt. must arrive at $\hat{7}$ (the leading tone) as the upbeat of that same penultimate bar. The final bar will then contain an octave or unison on the tonic. (Compare the first species.) Note that these rules insure against doubling the leading tone, which is prohibited, because the double resolution to $\hat{1}$ produces parallel octaves.

a) The upper ctpt. must proceed $\hat{6}$ to $\hat{7}$ in the penultimate bar against the $\hat{2}$ of the cantus firmus. (Example: penultimate bar contains half notes B4-C♯5 against a CF E4; the final bar contains the octave D5 against D4.) In the minor mode, ↑6 and ↑7 must be used.

b) The lower ctpt. must proceed $\hat{5}$ to $\hat{7}$ in the penultimate bar against the $\hat{2}$ of the cantus firmus. (Example: the penultimate bar contains half notes A3-C♯4 against a CF E4; the final bar contains the unison D4 against D4.) Again, in the minor mode, ↑7 must be used.

14. A whole-note leading tone in the ctpt. may be used in the penultimate bar if the standard cadence given in rule #13 is awkward or impossible. In this instance, the cadence is identical to the first-species cadence.

Preferences and Hints

15. Maintain a balance between consonant and dissonant upbeats. Recall that you can skip from a consonance but must treat a dissonance as a passing tone in stepwise motion.

16. Keep the ctpt. fluid and clearly directed through a balance of skips and steps. Too many skips will make the exercise sound

choppy. Nothing but stepwise motion in the ctpt. may be monotonous, but too many steps are better than too many skips. Strive also to balance consonant and dissonant passing tones.

17. Because of the restrictions on the use of dissonance, second species can often be tricky to correct or improve: one must sometimes rewrite two or three bars in order to correct a single error. Again, it is often easier to work backwards from the cadence after establishing the beginning.

18. Build the ctpt. to a high point, then descend to the cadence.

Exercises

Continue to label all the intervals in the exercise. Place the interval numbers between the staves. Align the music correctly so that the attacks of simultaneous notes appear in a vertical line.

Continue to place triangles around the interval numbers of perfect consonances. In addition, *circle* the interval numbers of the dissonant intervals. This will provide another visual check for the exercise: be sure that any circled interval is a passing tone, i.e., that the second-species part approaches and leaves the dissonance by stepwise motion in the same direction. Further, remember to check the triangles: they must begin and end the exercise, two in a row is weak or an error, and any interval marked by a triangle must not be approached through similar motion.

Triangles may appear *within* bars using oblique motion. If there are not too many, they may not be weaknesses.

Visually assess the exercise by observing the relationships among circles, triangles, and unmarked interval numbers (imperfect consonances). The most important point is that there should not be too many triangles. Strive for a substantial number of circles (dissonances) as well.

Check the notation of the exercise to be sure it looks smooth. It should never be monotonous (returning to the same note or group of notes). Remember to build gently to a high point, then descend to the cadence.

Complete the following exercises in the two-part second species. As always, do at least one upper and lower ctpt. for each CF assigned. Recall that it is possible transpose the CF in order to place it in a proper range for a chosen voice.

Exercise 3-1: the Fux D-minor CF: D4 - F4 - E4 - D4 - G4 - F4 - A4 - G4 - F4 - E4- D4

Exercise 3-2: A♭3 - F4 - D♭4 - E♭4 - F4 - G4 - B♭4 - A♭4 - E♭4 - D♭4 - B♭3 - A♭3 (in A♭ major)

Exercise 3-3: B3 - D4 - E4 - F♯4 - G♯4 - A♯4 - B4 - F♯4 - D4 - C♯4 - B3 (in B minor)

Chapter 4

Two-Part Third Species
(Four Notes Against One)

[Schenker 1, 227–56]

This species consists of four quarter notes in the ctpt. against a whole note in the CF.

Except for the *nota cambiata* (defined below in rule #17), the third species does not contain new material; instead, the study of passing tones, introduced in the second species, continues. The third species presents fewer problems than does the second, because the greater number of notes per bar allows one to work out of tight spots more easily. Revision is simpler with less large-scale rewriting than in the second species.

Absolutes

1. Downbeats must be consonant, as in the first and second species.

2. Dissonant or consonant quarter notes may occur on the second, third, or fourth quarter of the bar.

23

3. When a dissonant pitch occurs on the third quarter of the bar (i.e., on the upbeat), an *accented passing tone* is created. Its dissonance carries more weight than dissonances on the second and fourth quarters (since it is stronger metrically), but the accented passing tone is not treated in any special manner.

4. As in second species, dissonant pitches must be approached and left by step in the same direction (with the *nota cambiata* an exception [rule #17]).

5. Dissonant pitches in the ctpt. must occur between two different consonant pitches; i.e., each dissonant pitch must be a passing tone. Two permissible exceptions: 1) against a leading tone $\hat{7}$ in the CF, the quarter notes $\hat{5}$-$\hat{4}$-$\hat{3}$-$\hat{2}$ in the upper ctpt: the *two* middle quarter notes are dissonances; 2) in the minor mode, with a $\hat{3}$ in the CF, the quarter notes $\hat{5}$-$\hat{\flat6}$-$\hat{\sharp7}$-$\hat{1}$ in either the lower or upper ctpt.: the *two* middle quarter notes are dissonances. Note that the dissonances are still approached and left by step in the same direction (rule #4).

6. As in the second species, dissonant neighboring tones are to be avoided for pedagogical purposes. They are too easy to apply; their overuse also creates a static effect.

7. Consonant quarter notes may be approached and left by skip.

8. Avoid too many large leaps. As in all species melodic writing, a large skip should be followed by stepwise motion in the opposite direction.

9. Avoid more than two skips in a row, if possible (even small ones). These create arpeggiations, which mostly should be avoided in such active lines. This is a refinement of the rules of melodic writing from chapter 1.

10. As usual, the beginning must be a perfect consonance, but not the lower fifth.

11. The ctpt. should begin with a quarter rest. As in the second species, this effect creates more momentum than a joint attack, with the CF, of the downbeat. The first quarter note must still be a perfect consonance.

12. Four temporal relationships characterize third species: a) fourth quarter to the following downbeat, b) third quarter (upbeat) to the following downbeat, c) downbeat to the following downbeat, and d) upbeat to the following upbeat. Each case in turn:

a) Between the fourth quarter and the downbeat, similar motion and parallel motion to perfect consonances are prohibited. This relationship should be treated as in the first and second species.

b) Between the third quarter (the upbeat) and the downbeat, parallel perfect consonances should generally be avoided, although if a leap larger than a third to the fourth quarter occurs, the result may be permissible.

c) Between downbeats, parallel perfect consonances should generally be avoided, although such a motion may be used if the intervening three quarter notes sufficiently compensate the effect.

d) Between upbeats (i.e., from a third quarter to a third quarter), parallel perfect consonances may be used, generally without restriction. When aurally conspicuous, they are called *afterbeat* octaves and fifths.

13. Avoid the awkward *faulty third leap*. This occurs when three or four stepwise pitches are followed by the leap of a third, *in the same direction*, into the downbeat of the next bar. Leaps larger than a third are even worse.

14. Cadences: since the CF will resolve $\hat{2}$-$\hat{1}$, the ctpt. must arrive at the leading tone on the fourth quarter of the penultimate bar,

then resolve to either the octave or unison on the final bar. (Compare first and second species.)

15. There are several possibilities for approaching the leading tone at the fourth quarter of the penultimate bar, but avoid parallel octaves or unisons from the upbeat to the downbeat. For example, consider the quarter notes B4-C5-D5-B4 against D4 in the CF resolving to C5 against C4 in the CF: We hear the parallel octaves of D5-D4 on the penultimate bar's upbeat moving to C5-C4.

16. Avoid isolated and seemingly arbitrary skips in passages that are mostly stepwise (scalar). They are usually awkward.

Preferences and Hints

17. The *nota cambiata* (in English, a "cambiata") may be used without restriction in a third-species line. (Its Italian plural is *note cambiate*.) This effect combines two passing motions within five notes and is the only time in species exercises when a dissonance may be freely skipped *from*. Dissonances may never be skipped *to* (with, arguably, minor exceptions in complicated combinations of species treated in later chapters).

    a) Definition of the *nota cambiata*:
        (1) first note consonant
        (2) second note dissonant, approached stepwise, left by third *in the same direction*
        (3) third note consonant
        (4) fourth note returns in the opposite direction by step, thus continuing the passing motion from second note
        (5) last note consonant and completes the step motion of the third and fourth notes

b) The cambiata may go from first quarter to first quarter or third quarter to third quarter. No other possibilities are allowed.

c) Example of descending cambiata in upper ctpt.: E4 in the CF against E5 to D5 (dissonance skipped from) to B4 to C5 to D5 (against B3 in cantus firmus). This combines two interlocked passing motions: E5-D5-C5 and B4-C5-D5.

d) Example of ascending cambiata in upper ctpt.: C4 in the CF against E4 to F4 (dissonance skipped from) to A4 to G4 to F4 (against D4 in the CF).

18. The ctpt. should be well-balanced and include steps, interesting leaps, *cambiate*, dissonant passing tones on the third quarter, etc.

19. The desiderata from rule #18 should yield a line that is supple, lyrical, and forward-moving. As usual, try and build to a climax, then descend.

Exercises

Continue to label intervals with triangles around perfect consonances and dissonances circled. *Review*: be careful of two triangles in a row; triangles should appear at the beginning and end; be sure triangles are not approached through similar motion; be sure circled intervals are passing tones. Mark each use of a *nota cambiata* with a bracket enclosing the five notes and labeled "n.c." Be sure each pitch in the cambiata is treated correctly.

Complete the following exercises in third species. Include at least one *nota cambiata* in each exercise. As usual, complete at least one upper and lower ctpt. for each CF.

Exercise 4-1: The Fux D-minor CF (D4 - F4- E4 - D4 - G4 - F4 - A4 - G4 - F4 - E4 - D4)

Exercise 4-2: A3 - E4 - F♯4 - G♯4 - A4 - E4 - F♯4 - D4 - C♯4 - B3 - A3 (in A major)

Exercise 4-3: F♯3 - C♯4 - A3 - D4 - C♯4 - D♯4 - E♯4 - F♯4 - B3 - A3 - G♯3 - F♯3 (in F♯ minor)

Chapter 5

Two-Part Fourth Species
(Syncopation)

[Schenker 1, 257–309]

This species consists of constant half-note syncopations in the ctpt. against the CF. That is, a half note on the upbeat is tied to a half note on the following downbeat. The tie to the downbeat in the ctpt. creates a *suspension*.

The suspended note may also be called a *syncopation* or *syncope*. It is syncopated at the point of attack and becomes a suspension at the following downbeat.

For the purposes of this book, the notation "sus" will be used to signify a suspended interval. For example, "sus4" means that the interval of a fourth is tied to and is thereby created in the ctpt. when the CF changes on the downbeat. A similar notation will be used for scale steps: "sus$\hat{4}$" means that $\hat{4}$ is being tied to.

Fux points out that there is a sense in which the fourth species is like the first species with the contrapuntal line displaced or shifted by a half note. That is, an exercise in the fourth species creates a rocking motion, a ping-pong effect of notes alternating between the two first-species lines offset by a half measure.

The fourth species comes across curiously to the modern ear, because a melody comprising *continuous* syncopations sounds artificial, even mechanical. However, suspensions used judiciously create an excellent musical effect. They work especially well when incorporated into the fifth (mixed) species and later in free composition.

Because continual suspensions spanning an exercise will usually not be possible, it is often necessary to switch briefly to the second species to gain new space or relieve monotony. This procedure will be elaborated in rule #12.

Absolutes

1. Begin, as usual, on a perfect consonance (excluding the lower fifth). The beginning of the exercise should be a half rest followed by a half note tied to a half note in the following bar to initiate the fourth-species rhythmic pattern.

2. In the fourth species, the ctpt. on the upbeat (tied *from*) must be consonant against the cantus firmus. (This was the case in rule #1 automatically.)

3. On the downbeat (tied *to*), the ctpt. may be either dissonant or consonant.

4. The dissonance tied to the downbeat creates a unique situation among the species: it is the only time when you can hear a dissonance at the downbeat of a bar, that is, at the moment when a note of the CF changes.

5. The dissonant suspension must resolve by step downward to a consonance on the upbeat, which is then tied to the following downbeat. This process creates a *chain* of suspensions. (The downward resolution by step in the fourth species recalls the second and third species in which passing-tone dissonances also resolve by step, although in either direction. In general, all dissonances in species counterpoint must be resolved by stepwise motion.)

6. It follows from rule #5 that the dissonant syncope must not resolve upward. Schenker attempts to justify why, but his reasons, based on viewing the syncopations as derived from dissonant passing tones, are more speculative than convincing. Fux merely asserts that downward resolution is standard practice—the reasons why being too difficult for the student to comprehend—and leaves it at that. Perhaps the best justification is that release of tension is best served by downward motion; because the species method is intended to be straightforward, downward resolution best satisfies this goal.

7. Unlike the dissonance at the downbeat (which must resolve downwards by step), the consonance at the downbeat may proceed by skip or step to the following upbeat (which in the fourth species must be consonant).

8. To summarize the preceding rules, remember that the suspension contains three parts:

1) the preparation—this occurs on the upbeat, which is tied *from* and *must* be consonant

2) the suspension itself—this occurs on the downbeat, which is tied *to* and may be either dissonant or consonant

3) the resolution (if the suspension was dissonant)—this occurs on the upbeat, resolving the dissonant suspension downward one step to a consonance. (Again, the consonant suspension needs no resolution and may be skipped from.) The resolution of the dissonant suspension, if tied from, creates a new suspension.

Take care not to get this process backwards by making the preparation dissonant and the suspension consonant.

9. A sus5-6 or sus6-5 progression creates a change of harmony within a bar. (Note again the use of "sus" on the interval number to indicate that the interval was created by a suspension; the

number after the hyphen signifies the interval after the suspended note proceeds to the next note. In the case of a dissonant
suspension it must resolve downward, as in sus4-3.)

10. The following enumeration summarizes the possible dissonant syncopes in the upper ctpt. They are then evaluated in terms
of their effect. Note that the best suspensions are those that resolve to the imperfect consonances, thirds and sixths.

> a) sus4-3. Excellent
> b) sus7-6. Excellent
> c) sus2-1. Use sparingly—empty resolution to the CF
> d) sus9-8. Use sparingly—empty resolution to the octave

11. The only possible dissonant syncopes in the lower ctpt. are:

> a) sus2-3. Excellent—in fact, the *only* good lower dissonant
> suspension that resolves convincingly to an imperfect conso-
> nance
> b) sus4-5. Use sparingly—"resolution" to the perfect fifth is
> weak
> c) sus7-8. Especially weak—must be avoided
> d) sus♭5-6. Questionable: when the fifth is diminished, the
> "resolution" is uncharacteristic of the tritone and should
> generally be avoided. (When the fifth is perfect, the down-
> beat is consonant, so there is in fact no resolution to the 6.
> This progression may be used freely.)

12. As in the second and third species, no notes may be repeated
in a fourth-species line. However, because fourth-species lines
tend to move downward (because of the required dissonance
resolutions), a good way to regain upper space is to leap an octave.

13. The syncopations may be interrupted momentarily. Doing so
can:

> a) relieve monotony

b) inject new energy into the line

c) effect a new continuation where none was possible

Interrupting the ties creates second-species settings. For the purposes of the exercise, only interrupt ties once or at most twice in an exercise, and then for only one or two notes. At the interruptions, write according to the rules of the second species and continue until you begin to syncopate anew (i.e., tie from the upbeat).

14. Four temporal relationships characterize the fourth species: a) upbeat to upbeat through a dissonant syncopation, b) upbeat to upbeat through a consonant syncopation, c) downbeat to downbeat, and d) a turn to the second species (when the ties are interrupted). Each case in turn:

a) From upbeat to upbeat through a dissonant syncopation, similar (and parallel) motion to a perfect consonance is not permitted. (Parallel imperfect consonances are typical of this species, as in a chain of sus4-3 suspensions.)

b) From upbeat to upbeat through a consonant downbeat, similar and even parallel motion to a perfect consonance may be used sparingly, though it can create a poor effect. Schenker feels that upbeat parallel fifths are preferable when ascending, as in the sequential 6-5 / sus6-5 motion with the lower ctpt., because the imperfect consonance is on the downbeat.

c) From downbeat to downbeat, similar motion to perfect consonances may be used, but only sparingly.

d) When the ties are interrupted, treat the exercise as if it were the second species; the voice-leading rules from that species then apply.

15. There are two possible cadences: in the upper ctpt. sus7-6 proceeding to an octave; in the lower ctpt. sus2-3 proceeding to a

unison. Note that in each instance the tonic pitch is prepared as a consonance, then becomes dissonant against the $\hat{2}$ of the CF in the penultimate bar. The dissonant tonic in the ctpt. resolves down to the leading tone, then up again to the tonic in the final bar.

Preferences and Hints

16. Imperfect consonances should be emphasized throughout the exercise. Yet, as usual, the first interval must be perfect (excepting the lower fifth), and the last an octave or unison.

17. Chains of resolutions to sixths or thirds are very common in the fourth species. Because of this, do not worry about the excessive parallel imperfect consonances that may result.

18. In the main body of the exercise, emphasize dissonant syncopations—they have more energy or forward motion—while including consonant syncopes for balance and variety.

19. As usual, try to maintain a balance between skips and steps. Despite your best efforts, however, fourth-species exercises will retain a certain mechanical quality.

Exercises

Continue to write your intervals and label with triangles or circles. In addition, write a tie *into* the number of a suspended interval. When checking, be sure your tied dissonances resolve downward by step. Include a hyphen ("-") between the interval numbers to show dissonance resolutions whenever they occur.

Note that with suspensions, two triangles in a row are not always weak. For example, you might resolve to a perfect consonance on the downbeat, then leap up an octave to the same perfect consonance on the upbeat. This figure will be symbolized by two triangles in a row, but creates no problems.

For each CF, write at least one lower and upper ctpt. in the fourth-species setting.

Exercise 5-1: The Fux D-minor CF (D4 - F4 - E4 - D4 - G4 - F4 - A4 - G4 - F4 - E4 - D4)

Exercise 5-2: F3 - C4 - A♭3 - D♭4 - C4 - E♮4 - F4 - B♭3 - C4 - A♭3 - G3 - F3 (in F minor)

Chapter 6

Two-Part Fifth Species
(Mixed Counterpoint)

[Schenker 1, 310–45]

The fifth species, the culmination of the study of two-part writing, enables us to write lines whose freedom approaches that of melodies found in free composition. More specifically, the fifth species is defined by a ctpt. that varies among the second, third, and fourth species supported by the CF.

The rules of each species apply to the activity of the contrapuntal line at that moment in the exercise when that species occurs. The only new material treated in the fifth species are the addition of eighth notes, principally as decorations, and the occurrences of more than one species in a single bar.

Absolutes

1. Begin the exercise with a half rest, then a half note, preferably tied (the fourth species). That is, the fourth species creates the best beginning for a mixed-species exercise.

2. Avoid beginning with the third species. It is preferable to build to a feeling of constant motion; with so little time in an

exercise, starting with third species may mean including too much of it or awkwardly halting the quarter-note motion midway.

3. Avoid the first species except for the last note of the exercise. In brief exercises, a whole note occurring anywhere else will interrupt the flow of the ctpt.

4. Avoid more than three half notes in succession when using the second species. A fourth half note, if syncopated (tied), is permissible.

5. Avoid more than three bars of continuous quarter notes.

6. Avoid isolated half notes within predominantly third-species passages. They sound awkward, rather like unexpected interruptions in what should be a smooth flow.

7. Eighth notes may be used to embellish a third-species passage, but only two at a time. Specifically, two eighth notes may be used on either the second or the fourth quarter beat of a given bar, but not on both (in the same bar). Avoid occasional eighth-note pairs used overtly as filler to complete quarter-note lines that come out a note "short."

8. The fifth species allows mixtures of the second, third, and fourth species *within* a single bar. The following new rules cover the special situations:

a) When a half note *is followed by* two quarter notes, either quarter note may be a dissonant or consonant passing tone.

b) When a half note *follows* two quarter notes, that half note must be consonant and tied to a quarter or half note in the next bar. (Pedagogical reasoning: because the effect of the rhythm is syncopated, an actual syncopation should result.)

c) The quarter note–half note–quarter note rhythm within a bar (a small-scale syncopation) must be avoided, because it is too complicated for the straightforward melodic lines found in generic sixteenth-century style.

d) Avoid two consecutive bars of half notes followed by two quarter notes. (In a species exercise, this rhythm can sound trite.)

9. Do not tie from a quarter note on the fourth beat. This will sound awkward because the suspension is insufficiently prepared and the rhythm too jerky.

10. A dotted half note followed by a quarter note must be avoided since this follows from no actual species type. (This is what Schenker claims, anyway. Note below [rule #13] that a three-beat duration may be obtained by tying a half note to a quarter note over the bar.)

11. The best cadence is taken from the fourth species, with or without a more decorated use of eighth notes. Example in the upper ctpt. in the key of F is as follows: against the CF A3 with F4 tied *from* in the ctpt. on the upbeat; the CF changes to G3 in the penultimate bar with the ctpt. F4 (quarter note, tied to) E4 (eighth note) D4 (eighth note) E4 (half note); the final bar is then F4-F3 (octave whole notes).

Preferences and Hints

12. Eighth notes are best in stepwise motion (and only on either the second or fourth quarter alone); use leaps with great care or avoid them entirely.

13. Care must be taken when a dissonant suspension is resolved by a quarter note on the second quarter of the bar. When this effect is used, the quarter note on the second beat must be conso-

nant with the CF and not effect a change of harmony. Leaps from this quarter-note resolution tend to be clumsy—the line is best continued stepwise, preferably downward. (When the syncope on the downbeat is consonant, the line may continue as usual on the second quarter note of the bar. This quarter note may be consonant, as a skip or step, or dissonant, in which case it must be a passing tone in stepwise motion.)

14. A simple eighth-note decoration of the second quarter note in the preceding rule is permissible. For example (in the upper ctpt.): CF is E; against it is susD (quarter note) C (eighth note) B (eighth note) C (half note). This construction delays the resolution of the suspension to the third quarter where it normally occurs. If the note attacked on the third quarter is a half note, it must be tied to the following bar (unless the exercise cadences).

15. An equilibrium should be maintained so that the exercise does not emphasize any one species in particular.

16. As usual, try to build the exercise to a high point, then descend to the cadence.

17. In this chapter, you may wish to begin experimenting with 3/2 time. The extensions of the rules are straightforward:

a) Dot the whole notes of the CF.

b) Tie the preparations for suspension from the third half-note beat.

c) A *nota cambiata* should begin on the second beat only, in order to conclude on the following downbeat.

d) As usual, any dissonances aside from suspensions should be passing tones.

e) Avoid the rhythm: two quarter notes followed by two half notes (in a given bar); that forbidden rhythm can often be rewritten (i.e., corrected) as two half notes followed by two quarter notes—a simpler, more straightforward continuation.

Exercises

Add at least one lower and upper ctpt. in the fifth species to the following CFs:

Exercise 6-1: The Fux D-minor CF (D4 - F4 - E4 - D4 - G4 - F4 - A4 - G4 - F4 - E4 - D4)

Exercise 6-2: B3 - C♯4 - E4 - D4 - F♯4 - G♯4 - A♯4 - B4 - E4 - D4 - C♯4 - B3 (in B minor)

Exercise 6-3: G3 - D4 - E♭4 - B♭3 - C4 - D4 - E♮4 - F♯4 - G4 - D4 - B♭3 - A3 - G3 (in G minor)

Part Two

Three-Part Counterpoint

Chapter 7

Three-Part First Species

[Schenker 2, 1–54]

The first species in three parts combines two contrapuntal lines in whole notes with the CF.

Three-part first species presents, for the first time, the possibility of writing complete triads. Three-part writing also permits the *doubling* of notes. For example, in a chord containing two Cs and one E, the Cs are said to be doubled and the chord is likely to be interpreted as an *incomplete triad* on C. Incomplete triads are thinner in sonority than complete triads, but are useful for voice-leading smoothness and as a balance to the greater richness of chords with three distinct notes.

Three-part counterpoint is usually written for three contiguous voices, that is, soprano-alto-tenor (SAT) or alto-tenor-bass (ATB). A soprano-alto-bass (SAB) combination is also possible. Although there may be considerable distance between the alto and bass parts, such a voicing is permissible and models instrumental situations where it is common. It is also possible to write for two voices of one type plus an adjacent voice: for example, soprano-soprano-alto or tenor-tenor-bass. In this arrangement, it is more common to have the higher voices be of the same type.

In general discussions and descriptions, I may call the top voice the *soprano*, the bottom the *bass*, and the middle the *alto*, *tenor*, or *inner voice*. The top two voices are sometimes distinguished from the bass and called the *upper voices* or *upper parts*.

43

The soprano and bass are often distinguished from the middle and called the *outer voices*. The outer voices (no matter how many inner parts) constitute the *two-voice framework* (see rule #20).

With the use of three parts, many of the intervals between the lowest and highest voice will extend beyond the octave. To label these most conveniently, use the actual interval number for any interval a twelfth (octave plus a fifth) or smaller. Beyond the twelfth, label intervals as if they were collapsed into an octave. For example, label a thirteenth as a sixth or a fifteenth as an octave. Chords are described by labeling the chordal intervals from the bass. The first number is the interval with the upper voice, while the second number defines the span to the middle voice. Hence, in a 6-3 chord, the upper voice forms a sixth with the bass and the middle voice forms a third with the bass.

Absolutes

Permissible Sonorities

1. In the first species, the three-part whole-note sonorities must *all* be consonant. A sonority is consonant when *all* of its intervals are consonant. One dissonant interval in the sonority renders the sonority dissonant.

2. When all three pitches are distinct, only root-position and first-inversion triads are permitted. The second-inversion triad forms the interval of a fourth (or compound fourth) with the bass and is dissonant, as elaborated in rule #3. Thus, second-inversion triads are dissonances and must be avoided in the first species.

3. The interval of a fourth is harmonically dissonant when it occurs between the bass and an upper voice, and thus always creates a dissonance. However, the fourth is a consonance when it occurs between the upper two parts, as in the first-inversion triad (see rule #2). (When a consonant fourth occurs between the up-

per parts, the interval number is not circled.) The forbidden use of the fourth with the bass voice parallels its dissonant status in two-part writing.

4. Root-position and second-inversion diminished triads are considered dissonances because tritones, as dissonant intervals, are present in the sonorities. However, the first inversion diminished triad *is* permissible, since the tritone is in the upper pair of voices. Thus the tritone between the upper two parts in a first-inversion diminished triad is not considered a dissonant interval and its interval number is not circled.

The previous four rules focus on sonorities with distinct (undoubled) pitches. Next, we treat incomplete triads and non-triadic sonorities.

5. Avoid a unison of all three parts.

6. If the outer parts form an octave, avoid doubling any of these notes with the inner voice. Likewise avoid a perfect fifth within (or on top of) an octave created by any two voices. (A perfect fifth within an octave could be used for the cadence if a medieval effect were desired.) Instead, use a third or sixth above the lowest part, for example, C4-E4-C5 or C4-A4-C5.

7. Doublings of the third or sixth above the bass (e.g., C3-A3-A4 or E3-G3-G4) may be used occasionally.

8. Avoid doubling the leading tone. This rule is often overlooked with three or more parts. Because each leading tone (in species writing) must resolve to the tonic, any joint resolutions create parallel octaves.

9. The following is a summary of the interval occurrences in the sonorities permissible in the main body of the exercise. (Recall that "open-fifth" sonorities should generally be avoided on downbeats except in rare instances at the beginning and cadence.)

a) The *third* (or *tenth*) occurs in four recommended sonorities: 5-3 (or 10-5) (e.g., C4-E4-G4 or C4-G4-E5); 6-3 (or 10-6) (e.g., C4-E4-A4 or C4-A4-E5); 8-3 (e.g., C4-E4-C5); and (less often) 10-3 (e.g., C4-E4-E5).

b) The *sixth* occurs in three recommended sonorities: 6-3 or 10-6 (e.g., C4-E4-A4 or C4-A4-E5); 8-6 or 6-8 (e.g., C4-A4-C5 or C4-C5-A5); and (less often) 6-6 (e.g., C3-A3-A4).

c) The *octave* occurs in two permissible sonorities: 8-3 (e.g., C4-E4-C5) and 8-6 (e.g., C4-A4-C5).

d) The *fifth* occurs in two recommended sonorities: 5-3 or 10-5 (e.g., C4-E4-G4 or C4-G4-E5) and 10-6 (e.g., E3-C4-G4). The perfect fifth should be combined with an imperfect consonance to avoid the "open fifth" sound.

e) The *fourth* occurs in one permissible sonority: 6-3 (e.g., E4-G4-C5).

f) The *augmented fourth* (tritone) and *diminished fifth* occur in one permissible sonority, the diminished triad in first inversion: 6-3 or 10-6 (e.g., D4-F4-B4 or D4-B4-F5).

Voice Leading

10. Voice crossing, when necessary, is permissible. It should not extend beyond one or (at most) two bars.

11. Avoid parallel fifths, octaves, and unisons between any pair of voices. Hence, it is necessary to check all three intervals in each progression (as opposed to one interval in two-part writing).

12. Similar motion to perfect fifths and octaves *is* frequently permissible. Compare its absolute avoidance in two-part writing. Thus we see an important consequence of dealing with three voices: the situations more closely resemble real music, and

hence rules that were simple and absolute in two-part writing start becoming fuzzier. Further, the additional texture provided by three parts often disguises weaknesses that are glaring in two parts. In general, the more parts that are involved in a texture, the less critical a weakness between any two parts becomes.

The rule, defined below, on similar motion to perfect intervals in three parts is complex but important, because these situations arise frequently in all multi-voice writing. The basic idea is that there are three criteria to be examined in any progression involving similar motion to a perfect interval; the more fully the criteria are satisfied, the better the progression will sound.

a) At least one of the three voices moves by a second, preferably the highest.

b) The second chord of the pair is a complete triad. (This condition is impossible to satisfy when the motion proceeds to a similar octave.)

c) The third voice (the one not involved in the questionable motion) proceeds in contrary motion. (Oblique motion in this voice will not help disguise the similar-motion progression.)

The three rules must be examined in turn when analyzing a progression involving similar motion:

• If all three criteria are positive, the motion is permissible.
• If all three criteria are negative, the motion is forbidden.
• Two out of three positive criteria means the motion will probably work.
• One out of three positive criteria means the motion will probably not work.

In these latter two instances, you must judge whether to keep or revise the progression. Contextual considerations (e.g., the extent to which the progression fits the entire exercise) will come into play and cannot be precisely specified.

13. Avoid anti-parallels between the outer voices.

14. The use of two major thirds linked by whole step is permissible if the resulting tritone is not too obvious.

15. Since the diminished fifth may be included in a sonority (rule #4), voice leading becomes possible between diminished and perfect fifths. These are permissible, because the prohibition of parallel fifths only applies to situations in which both fifths are perfect.

16. Avoid cross relations. These are more problematic in multipart writing. Because the vertical range of the exercise is larger, there is a greater chance of overlooking clashes between chromatic versions of the same note occurring in different registers.

Beginning and Cadence

17. A complete or incomplete tonic triad must occur at the beginning and end of the exercise. At the end, the tonic triad must also be in root position; at the beginning, the use of a non-root position tonic triad is acceptable if it helps avoid a difficult problem. Incomplete tonic triads normally contain doubled root and third; the sonority with doubled root and fifth should be avoided.

18. The penultimate bar must either use a V triad or the diminished vii chord in first inversion (vii^6). Accordingly, the cadences proceeding from the penultimate bar to the final bar must be formed in the following manner:

a) If the cantus ($\hat{2}$) is in an upper voice, then the bass must either proceed $\hat{5}$-$\hat{1}$ or $\uparrow\hat{7}$-$\hat{1}$ (Raised $\hat{7}$ is shown because the $\hat{7}$ must be altered in the minor mode to become a leading tone.) These two possibilities in turn:

(1) If the bass proceeds $\uparrow\hat{7}$-$\hat{1}$, then the CF (necessarily) proceeds $\hat{2}$-$\hat{1}$, while the third part takes $\hat{5}$ in each bar.

(2) If the bass proceeds $\hat{5}$-$\hat{1}$, then the CF (necessarily) proceeds $\hat{2}$-$\hat{1}$, while the third part proceeds $\uparrow\hat{7}$-$\hat{1}$.

b) If the cantus ($\hat{2}$) is in the bass, then one ctpt. proceeds $\uparrow\hat{7}$-$\hat{1}$ while the other proceeds $\hat{4}$-$\hat{5}$ or $\hat{4}$-$\hat{3}$. (Use of the $\hat{4}$-$\hat{5}$ motion must not create parallel fifths.)

These cadences underlie all three-part species writing.

Preferences and Hints

19. Recall that pitches may be repeated in first-species melodic lines (compare two-part first species).

20. As pointed out in the introduction to this section, the outer voices create a *two-voice framework*. (The inner voice in effect fills out the two-voice texture of the outer voices.) Two-voice frameworks are critically important in composition of all kinds. The outer voices without the middle voice should create a satisfying two-part texture. The additional middle voice should add richness to what is already musically compelling.

21. Although successful two-voice frameworks underlie virtually all three-part exercises, it is usually better to compose all three parts at once. Large-scale revisions are often necessary when one adds a third part to an already complete two-voice framework.

22. As in two-part writing, it is often helpful to establish the cadence and work backward.

23. The soprano, the most prominent part, should have the strongest melody. The bass should be almost as well constructed. If any part can be less interesting, it is the middle voice.

24. In general, the intervallic distance between the bass and the middle voice should be greater than the distance between the

upper pair of voices. (Still, the distance between the bass and the inner voice should generally not exceed a tenth or at most a twelfth.) One should usually be able to play the top two parts with the right hand. If the left hand has to take the middle note too often, the spacing could probably be improved: upon revision, try to voice the middle part closer to the soprano.

25. Maintain intervallic variety in the two-voice framework throughout the exercise.

26. Maintain variety in the spacing of the parts. In particular, strive to balance complete triads with incomplete triads. If more than half of the triads are incomplete, then revise for a fuller texture.

27. As usual, try to build the exercise (the upper part in particular) to a high point, then descend to the cadence.

Exercises

Write your voices on three separate staves. Be sure the whole notes are aligned in each bar.

Continue to label the intervals. Recall that in the first species only consonant intervals are permissible. Hence, first-species exercises should contain only perfect consonances (enclosed by triangles) and imperfect consonances (unmarked).

Write the intervals of the top two parts between the staves of those parts. Each of the parts in the top two staves will also form an interval with the bass. Write the two intervals with the bass vertically under the bass note: the upper number as the interval with the top voice, the lower number as the interval with the middle voice. These interval designations will resemble figured-bass notation, common in the baroque era.

Remember that a fourth (or compound fourth) with the bass is dissonant. Therefore, any fourth occurring below the bass staff should be circled, then eliminated upon revision. A fourth between the top two parts is permissible in a first-inversion triad, i.e., when the bass intervals are 6-3. A tritone occurring between the top two parts of a first-inversion diminished triad is a consonance, and therefore should not be circled. However, call attention to its status as a consonant tritone by labeling it either 4+ or 4+TT or 5- or 5-TT, depending on whether it is an augmented (sharp) fourth or diminished (flat) fifth. Be sure that two triangles in a row never occur in your interval numbers (in the first species).

Complete the following CFs in three-part first species. For each CF, write three versions: the CF first as the bass, then as an alto or tenor, then as the soprano voice. As usual, you may transpose the CF so that it fits the proper range of the intended part. For example, the Fux D-minor CF as the bass part could be transposed down an octave; as a soprano part, it could be transposed up a fifth to the key of A minor.

Exercise 7-1: The Fux D-minor CF (D4 - F4- E4 - D4 - G4 - F4 - A4 - G4 - F4 - E4 - D4)

Exercise 7-2: E4 - G♯4 - B4 - A4 - C♯5 - D♯5 - E5 - B4 - G♯4 - F♯4 - E (in E major)

Exercise 7-3: C4 - E♭4 - A♭4 - G4 - B♮4 - C5 - G4 - F4 - E♭4 - D4 - C4 (in C minor)

Chapter 8

Three-Part Second Species

[Schenker 2, 55–72]

This species consists of a second-species ctpt. and a first-species ctpt. written against the CF. *Simple* three-part species in general consists of one ctpt. in the new species while the second ctpt. and the CF remain in the first species. *Combined species*, introduced in the next chapter, contains multiple ctpts. of various species.

Absolutes

1. The permissible consonant sonorities, enumerated in the previous chapter, are the same for all species exercises. These occur on downbeats in the second species. Dissonant sonorities usually consist of incomplete seventh chords. (See rule #10.)

2. The voice-leading principles established in two-part second species continue to apply. In particular, passing-tone dissonances may occur on the upbeats. As passing tone dissonances, they must be approached and left by step in the *same* direction. Consonances on the upbeats may be approached and left by skip in any direction. Recall that notes may not be repeated in second-species melodies.

3. The exercise should begin with a half rest in the second-species part.

4. The exercise must begin with a complete or incomplete tonic triad, perferably in root position, and cadence with a complete or incomplete tonic triad in root position.

5. As in two-part species, the rules of motion governing downbeat-to-downbeat motion in the first species applies to upbeat-to-downbeat motion in the second species. Hence, continue (as always) to avoid parallel motion between perfect consonances in approaching the downbeat. This will apply to both the second-species and first-species lines.

6. Similar motion to perfect downbeat intervals should be examined for acceptability according to the three criteria established for three-part first species. (See chapter 7, rule #12.)

7. Parallel fifths and octaves between consecutive downbeats may occur in the second-species part. However, this motion should be disguised, preferably by an inner voice that leaps a third on the upbeat. For example, the first-species parts F4 over D3 proceed to E4 over C3, while the (inner-voice) second species proceeds A3-F3-G3. The downbeat parallel fifths (D3-A3 to C3-G3) are not particularly apparent.

8. Cadences (all examples treat the penultimate bar):

a) When the CF is not in the bass and the leading tone is in a first-species part, the second-species part can provide $\hat{5}$ (creating a dominant triad) with an octave leap in the penultimate bar. This results in a tripled tonic in the final bar, which is acceptable for a final sonority.

b) Do not allow the second-species voice to cadence $\hat{↑7}$-$\hat{5}$-$\hat{1}$, because the leading tone does not proceed, as it must, directly to the tonic.

c) Avoid creating a tritone between the leading tone on the second-species upbeat with $\hat{4}$ in the bass proceeding to the tonic. The leading tone is dissonant and the $\hat{4}$-$\hat{1}$ motion in the bass implies a IV-I harmonic progression. For example, if F3 is a first-species part in the bass and D4 is a first-species part in the alto, which proceed to E4 over C3, a second-species soprano with A4-B4-C5 does not create a suitable cadence. A consonant leading tone (against $\hat{2}$ in the bass) works well, on the other hand. For example, if the first-species parts in the proceeding example are exchanged, we obtain F4 over D3 to E4 over C3 supporting A4-B4-C5 in the second-species part. The B4 is consonant against the D3 in the bass, creating the implication of a vii⁶-I cadence.

d) If necessary, a fourth-species cadence can be used; i.e., the second-species part should be suspended as sus$\hat{8}$-$\hat{7}$-$\hat{8}$. This cadence will be further examined in chapter 12.

9. Continue to avoid cross relations, observe the rules of good melody writing, and be sure the soprano and bass (the two-voice framework) create a mostly satisfactory exercise without the inner voice.

Preferences and Hints

10. The dominant-seventh chord originates as a passing motion between dominant and tonic: for example, the first-species parts proceed B3 over G3 to C4 over C3, while the second-species line proceeds G4-F4-E4. The F4 is a dissonant passing tone. Hearing it as a harmonic entity provides a G dominant-seventh chord on the upbeat.

11. More generally, when the upbeat is a dissonant passing tone, then the downbeat harmony is considered *prolonged*. This important musical effect in free composition presents the simplest example of *composing-out*. (Prolongation and composing-out

also occur in one- and two-part writing, but are clarified in three parts because of the complete harmonies.)

12. The harmony established at the downbeat is generally heard as prolonged through a consonant upbeat, though ambiguities may arise, especially when triads are incomplete. An exception is the case of 5-6 or 6-5 in the second-species ctpt. (For example, first-species parts E4 over C4, while the second species proceeds G4-A4: the harmony can be heard as changing from C major to A minor [in first inversion] on the upbeat.)

13. In the main body of the exercise, continue with the usual mixture of consonant and dissonant passing tones, skips and steps in the second-species line, a balance between complete and incomplete triads, a soprano line with a strong melodic curve, etc.

Exercises

Continue to label your intervals as described in the chapter on three-part first species. Circle dissonant intervals and check afterwards to be sure they are passing tones.

Write at least three exercises for each CF. Rotate the CF and the second-species ctpt. into different parts. There are in fact six possibilities for ordering the two ctpts. with the CF. If we label the first-species ctpt. "1" and the second-species ctpt. "2," these possibilities are:

Top:	CF	CF	1	2	1	2
Middle:	1	2	CF	CF	2	1
Bottom:	2	1	2	1	CF	CF

You may find that it is most difficult to set the second-species part in the middle voice with the CF in the bass (the fifth option given).

Exercise 8-1: The Fux D-minor CF (D4 - F4- E4 - D4 - G4 - F4 - A4 - G4 - F4 - E4 - D4)

Exercise 8-2: Bb3 - Db4 - Gb5 - F4 - G♮4- A♮4 - Bb4 - F4 - Db4 - C4 - Bb3 (in Bb minor)

Chapter 9

Combined Counterpoint of the Second Species

[Schenker 2, 178–87]

Recall that "simple species" consists of exercises in which only one part is written in a species other than the first species. Accordingly, in "combined species" at least two parts appear in species other than the first species. The first combination to be explored consists of two second-species lines against the CF.

Because two notes proceed to the upbeat rather than one, three-part combined second species offers a wider range of harmonic behavior in a bar than is possible in the simple second species. In particular, the upbeat may continue a harmony stated or implied at the downbeat or it may change the harmony entirely.

Absolutes

1. All standard voice-leading prohibitions, cross relations, and rules of melodic structure remain in force.

2. Each line in the second-species setting observes the rules of individual second-species lines. Hence, the downbeat sonorities

must be consonant and all dissonances occurring on the upbeats must be passing tones.

3. The key rule for the combined second species: all half-note upbeats in the ctpts. must be consonant with each other. Although each upbeat in the ctpts. may be dissonant with the CF (and hence must be treated as a passing tone), the two second-species upbeats must remain internally consonant.

4. Take care to avoid fourths and tritones between the upbeat second-species parts unless they are made consonant by the CF (as first-inversion triads).

5. Avoid the second formed by intervals 5 and 6 with the CF: each line may be consonant with the CF, but the interval of the second between the second-species lines is internally dissonant.

6. The voice-leading rules of the combined second-species setting can be broken up into strict and less strict forms. Use the less strict rule if you are confident that a passage works well. Otherwise, rely on the stricter approach.

a) The strict approach: if a half-note upbeat in one ctpt. is dissonant with the CF, the upbeat in the other ctpt., even if it is consonant with the CF, must also be approached by step and left by step.

b) The less strict approach: a consonant upbeat in one line (occurring with a dissonant upbeat in the other) may be *arrived at* through a consonant leap. When both upbeats *continue* by step, the passage will usually work well. A leap *from* the consonant upbeat is often weak, though it may be possible. Each instance must be analyzed separately; as usual, contextual considerations render it impossible to enumerate all possibilities.

In either case, the line with the dissonant upbeat must always proceed by step, and the upbeats in the two ctpts. must remain consonant with each other.

Preferences and Hints

7. A dissonant neighboring tone may be included discreetly in one of the second-species lines, but it is preferable when combined with (i.e., disguised by) a passing tone in the alternate second-species line.

8. Recall that it is permissible in second-species writing to use a first-species cadence with a whole note in the penultimate bar. This rule may be extended to combined second-species settings where either part or both may take a whole note in the penultimate bar.

9. In writing cadences, remember that the leading tone in the penultimate bar must not be dissonant.

10. It is helpful to note that the combined second-species setting presents a two-part first-species setting in "double time." That is, the two second-species lines proceed together in consonances for the entire exercise. (Of course, some of their consonances, such as fourths, may depend upon a bass note given in the CF.)

11. The combined second-species setting presents a very important principle useful in orchestration: parts proceeding together as a unit (say, a saxophone section in a big band or woodwinds in an orchestra) should be internally consonant even if they are dissonant against slower moving parts. Indeed, the combined second-species setting can be used to practice this principle of orchestration.

Exercises

For each CF, write at least three exercises in the combined second species. For each setting, the CF should be placed in a different voice.

Exercise 9-1: The Fux D-minor CF (D4 - F4- E4 - D4 - G4 - F4 - A4 - G4 - F4 - E4 - D4)

Exercise 9-2: C♯4 - E4 - G♯4 - F♯4 - G♯4 - A♯4 - B♯4 - C♯5 - G♯4 - F♯4 - D♯4 - C♯4 (in C♯ minor)

Chapter 10

Three-Part Third Species

[Schenker 2, 73–82]

This species presents a setting of four quarter notes in the third-species part against a first-species ctpt. and the CF.
Schenker points out that with the possibility of two passing tones within the bar (connecting the first to the fourth quarter), a harmony may be composed out through the span of a fourth, (rather than the more typical third spans encountered with passing tones). For example, consider C3-E4 (whole notes) supporting G4-A4-B4-C5 in the third species: A4 and B4 are passing tones that compose out the C-major harmony.

Absolutes

Three-part third species presents no new problems; the accumulated rules apply directly. In particular, review the rules for two-part third species (chapter 4). Some of the rules most often overlooked are summarized in the rules that follow.

1. Avoid the running third leap to the downbeat, e.g., quarter notes G4-A4-B4-C5 leading to E5. Skips larger than a third are also impermissible.

2. As in two-part third-species settings, dissonant neighboring notes in the third-species part should be avoided, because they are too easy to use.

3. The criteria for successful similar motion to perfect consonances on downbeats continue to apply (chapter 7, rule #12).

4. The parallel- and similar-motion rules involving consecutive upbeats or downbeats from two-part third species continue to apply. Note that the parallels arising from downbeat chords can be permissible if the quarter notes in between the downbeats soften the effect. Also such parallels, if hidden in the lower voices, may be naturally unobtrusive.

5. The cadence rules are again as in two-part third-species settings. However, avoid:

   a) leaping to the leading tone on the downbeat of the penultimate bar

   b) treating the leading tone as a dissonance: e.g., E4 (CF) and G3 (whole note) supporting G4-A4-B4-C♯5 (leading tone; dissonant to the G bass) and cadencing to D3-D4-D5. As in the comparable second-species situation (see chapter 8, rule #8c), this cadence implies a subdominant-to-tonic motion.

Preferences and Hints

6. Try to use a variety of dissonant and consonant passing tones on the third quarter especially, which is the most emphasized rhythmic value in the bar (excepting the downbeat).

7. Recall the *nota cambiata*, the third-species musical figure that allows a skip from a dissonance. The following is a cadence formula that incorporates the *nota cambiata*: E4-G4 (whole

notes) supporting E5-D5 (dissonant skip in the same direction to:)-B4-C♯4 (four quarters) to D4-F4-D5. The *nota cambiata* may only proceed from downbeat to downbeat or upbeat (third quarter) to upbeat.

8. In general, larger skips (fifths or octaves) sound better when made to notes on the second or fourth quarter of the bar. Since the first and third quarters receive rhythmic emphasis naturally, skipping to them as well is often heavy-handed.

9. Strive for fluency in the construction of the third-species lines: they should flow freely, build to satisfying climaxes, and cadence gracefully.

10. Be sure to follow the standard rules of melody writing and avoid cross relations.

Exercise

Complete at least three versions for the following CF. As usual, the CF and the third-species part should be placed in a different voice each time. Label your intervals and bracket any use of the *nota cambiata*.

Exercise 10-1: The Fux D-minor CF (D4 - F4- E4 - D4 - G4 - F4 - A4 - G4 - F4 - E4 - D4)

Chapter 11

Combined Counterpoints of the Second and Third Species

[Schenker 2, 191–99]

For three-part counterpoints, the principal combination consists of one second-species line and one third-species line against the CF. A secondary combination consists of two third-species lines against the CF. Its rules are also given below.

As we have seen earlier, the third-species setting allows a possible dissonant passing tone on the upbeat of the bar. This potential third-quarter dissonance, in interacting with the second-species half note, can be approached from a more or less strict perspective. In the less strict approach, a third-quarter dissonance may be allowed between the third quarter note and the upbeat half note. This is the first time in species exercises that the possibility of attacking a dissonance without preparation is permitted. The stricter approach rules this out. Both are compared below.

Absolutes

1. All standard voice-leading prohibitions, cross relations, cadences, and rules of melodic structure remain in force. In gen-

64

eral, each ctpt. in the second and third species must obey its customary rules relative to the CF. The new material concerns how the ctpts. interact. Among the new situations that arise in this combination are potential (and, as usual, forbidden) parallel perfect consonances between the second and third species within or at the end of a bar.

2. In the strict approach to this combination, passing tones from the second and third species coinciding on the upbeat must be consonant with each other (although each may be dissonant with the CF).

3. In the less strict approach, the third quarter note of the bar may be dissonant with the upbeat half note. This effect works best when:

   a) the upbeat half note is consonant with the CF
   b) the upbeat half note extends the downbeat harmony
   c) the dissonance is not an interval of a second

Gradual deviation from these criteria weakens the effectiveness of the passage. If a third-quarter dissonance seems to work well with the second-species line, it may be worth keeping. Otherwise, it is safer to stay with the stricter rule.

Preferences and Hints

4. The second-species part may have to leap more often to accommodate the third-species quarter notes. While musically unappealing (especially when the second-species part is the soprano), it is often unavoidable.

5. In general, fluency in the second-species part may be sacrificed for the sake of the third-species part.

Rules for Two Third-Species Lines Against the CF (Optional)

6. The lines should avoid excessive parallel thirds and sixths.

7. The lines must remain consonant with each other, even if both are dissonant with the cantus firmus.

8. Use of the *nota cambiata* is possible, but the two third-species lines must remain consonant with each other.

Exercises

Continue to label intervals. Besides checking for the usual problems, note especially circled dissonances occurring between the second- and third-species parts on the upbeats (the less strict approach). Unless these moments work well, revise.

For each CF, write at least three exercises in three-part combined second and third species. For each version, place the CF and each species in a different voice. (There are six possibilities for ordering the voices.)

Exercise 11-1: The Fux D-minor CF (D4 - F4- E4 - D4 - G4 - F4 - A4 - G4 - F4 - E4 - D4)

Exercise 11-2: F4 - A♭4 - B♭4 - C5 - D♮5 - E♮5 - F5 - D♭5 - C5 - B♭4 - G4 - F4 (in F minor)

Chapter 12

Three-Part Fourth Species

[Schenker 2, 83–117]

The fourth-species setting in three parts consists of syncopated half notes in one part against a first-species ctpt. and the CF. Syncopes in the upper two parts are conceived and named in relation to the bass. Syncopes in the bass are conceived and named in relation to both upper parts. The addition of a third part fills out the chord, which can help improve certain suspensions that did not work well in two parts (see rule #6). The "upper" suspension may actually occur in either the middle or upper part, but for the illustrations below, the soprano part is chosen as bearing the suspension.

Absolutes

1. All standard voice-leading prohibitions, cross relations, and rules of melodic writing remain in force.

2. Recall that the suspension has three parts: preparation, syncopation, and (if dissonant) resolution. The preparation and resolution must be consonant. The syncopation itself may be consonant or dissonant.

3. If dissonant, the syncope must resolve downward by step to a consonance.

4. Consonant syncopes need not resolve and so can be skipped from.

5. The resolution tones must not be doubled or anticipated in the first-species part. The psychological basis for this rule is as follows: giving away the resolution of the dissonant suspension robs the suspension of its force. For example, against a sus7-6 suspension in the upper voice, the middle voice must not sustain 6. There are two common exceptions to this rule, as will be seen in rule #6.

6. The best dissonant syncopes in the upper ctpts. are sus4-3 and sus7-6. The sus9-8 syncope can also be used, especially if the first-species voice fills out the harmony, for example if the third or sixth is sustained by that voice. To summarize the dissonant syncopes in the upper ctpts.:

sus7-6		sus9-8	
3	*excellent*	3	*good*
sus7-6		sus9-8	
8	*good*	6	*OK*
sus4-3		sus9-8	
5	*excellent*	5	*avoid*
sus4-3		sus4-3	
8	*good*	6	*good*

These syncopations are ranked based on the resolution harmonies. Excellent resolutions give rise to complete triads, i.e., a 6-3 or 5-3 chord. The dissonant syncope to avoid resolves to an 8-5 "chord," or open octave and fifth. Note that the sus9-8 suspensions *do* anticipate the notes of resolution, but the suspensions are usable because the third part improves what is the very weak sus9-8 suspension in two parts.

7. The best dissonant syncope in the lower ctpt. is sus2-3. A sus4-5 syncope can also be used, especially if the third voice completes the harmony. (Recall that this suspension is weak in two-part writing.) To summarize the dissonant syncopes in the bass:

sus4-5		sus9-10	
sus2-3	*excellent*	sus2-3	*possible*
sus5-6			
sus2-3	*excellent*		

8. A sus5-6 / sus5-6 progression in the lower ctpt. must be avoided if there is a resolution to a 6-4 (second-inversion) triad.

9. Strive for a V-I progression at the cadence. As discussed earlier, the best cadence suspends the tonic pitch into the penultimate bar as a dissonance; the dissoant Î then resolves down by step to a consonant leading tone, then to Î on the final bar (as a consonance, of course). Follow the rules for the two-part fourth species cadences.

Preferences and Hints

10. As usual, the two-voice framework remains important in determining the fundamental quality of the exercise.

11. At the beginning of the exercise, a syncope may be omitted in the first bar if necessary.

12. Chains of afterbeat fifths are possible and, according to Schenker, often produce a good effect. They seem best when unobtrusive.

13. Since there is really only one good cadence (rule #9), it is often best to write it in as you begin the exercise. Then work backwards from this cadence.

14. Recall that in order to work out of a tight spot, regain space, or relieve monotony, the ties may be interrupted momentarily. When the upbeat is not tied, the rules of three-part second-species settings apply.

Exercises

Exercise 12-1: The Fux D-minor CF (D4 - F4 - E4 - D4 - G4 - F4 - A4 - G4 - F4 - E4 - D4)

Exercise 12-2: E4 - G4 - B4 - G4 - A4 - C5 - B4 - A4 - G4 - F♯4 - E4 (in E minor)

Chapter 13

Three-Part Mixed Species

[Schenker 2, 118–123]

This species consists of a mixed ctpt. (incorporating second, third, and fourth species) against a first-species ctpt. and the CF.

As in the two-part mixed (or fifth) species, the goal is to construct a melodic line that sounds freely composed.

The following rules mostly duplicate those of two-part mixed species and pertain to the voice written in the mixed species format. The two first-species parts follow the conventions already established for three-part species.

Absolutes

1. Avoid the first species in the mixed-species part except for the last note of the exercise.

2. The rules of each species apply to the current activity of the mixed-species line.

3. Avoid more than three half notes in succession in the mixed-species line. A fourth half note, if syncopated (tied), is permissible.

4. Avoid more than three bars of continuous (third-species) quarter notes in the mixed-species line.

5. Avoid isolated half notes within predominantly third-species passages. They sound awkward, rather like unexpected interruptions in what should be a smooth flow.

6. Eighth notes may be used to embellish a third-species passage, but only two at a time. Specifically, two eighth notes may be used on either the second or the fourth quarter beat of a given bar, but not on both (in the same bar). The correlate to rule #5: avoid occasional eighth-note pairs used to fill in quarter-note lines that come out a note "short."

7. The fifth species allows combinations of the second, third, and fourth species within a single bar. Note the following:

a) When a half note is followed by two quarter notes, either quarter may be a dissonant or consonant passing tone.

b) When a half note follows two quarter notes, that half note must be tied to a quarter or half note in the next bar. (Because the effect of the rhythm is syncopated, an actual syncopation should result.)

c) The quarter note–half note–quarter note rhythm within a bar (a small-scale syncopation) must be avoided, because it is too complicated for straightforward melodic lines in generic sixteenth-century style.

d) Avoid two consecutive bars of a half note followed by two quarter notes.

8. A dotted half note followed by a quarter note must be avoided, because this rhythm arises from no actual species construction. A three-beat duration, however, may be obtained by tying a half note to a quarter over the bar.

9. Begin the exercise with a half rest, then a half note, preferably tied (the fourth species). Avoid a third-species beginning; instead, build to a feeling of motion.

10. The best cadence is the fourth species, with or without a more decorated use of eighth notes. Example in the lower ctpt.: CF and first species G4 and C4; susF3 (quarter) E3 (eighth) D3 (eighth) E3 (half); final bar: whole notes F3-A3-F4.

Preferences and Hints

11. Eighth notes are best in stepwise motion (and only on either the second or fourth quarter alone); use leaps with great care or avoid them entirely.

12. A dissonant suspension may be resolved by a quarter note on the second quarter of the bar. It must be consonant with the CF and not effect a change of harmony. Leaps from this quarter-note resolution tend to be clumsy—the line is best continued stepwise, preferably downward.

13. A simple eighth-note decoration of the second quarter note in the preceding rule is permissible. Example in the upper ctpt.: CF and first species E3 and G3; susD4 (quarter) C4 (eighth) B3 (eighth) C4 (half). This decoration places the resolution of the suspension on the third quarter where it normally occurs. If the note attacked on the third quarter is a half note, it must be tied to the following bar (unless the exercise cadences).

14. An equilibrium should be maintained so that the exercise does not emphasize any one species in particular.

15. Remember not to tie from a quarter at the end of a bar.

Exercises

For each CF, write at least three versions. In each version, place the mixed-species line and CF in a different voice.

Exercise 13-1: The Fux D-minor CF (D4 - F4- E4 - D4 - G4 - F4 - A4 - G4 - F4 - E4 - D4)

Exercise 13-2: B3 - F♯4 - E4 - G4 - F♯4 - A♯4 - B4 - F♯4 - E4 - D4 - C♯4 - B3 (in B minor)

Chapter 14

Combined Species Incorporating Syncopation

[Schenker 2, 210–25, 228–42, 249–50]

This chapter treats the problem of combining the syncopated species with the second and third species.

The combinations are a) one fourth species and one second species and b) one fourth species and one third species. It is usually not feasible to create exercises with two (or more) fourth-species parts, because the downward resolution of multiple fourth-species dissonances is too restricting.

Incorporation of the second species provides new possibilities for the fourth-species dissonance resolutions. (I should emphasize that for the following exposition, the numbers given all refer to intervals, not scale steps.) For example, assume a sus7 (inner voice) and 12 (soprano) on a downbeat with the CF in the bass. The 12 in the soprano cannot be a whole note because the resolution of the sus7 downward to 6 creates a dissonance with that whole note; yet the 12 (or, within the octave, 5) as a second-species half note can proceed to 3 or 6 on the upbeat and so provide a consonant sonority for the resolution of the suspension.

Another instance of an unworkable three-part passage in the simple fourth species consists of the following: assume a 6 and sus5 on the downbeat with the CF as the soprano, the syncope in the middle, and a first-species part as the bass; when the sus5 (since it is a dissonant 2 with the CF) "resolves" downward, it creates a dissonant 4 with the bass. If, alternatively, the bass were a second-species line, that bass part might proceed up a step or down a third to avoid the dissonance. The moving second- or third-species lines can proceed to different notes, thereby opening up new possibilities for dissonance resolution.

If the CF is not in the bass, the syncope's interval of resolution may differ from the norm; e.g., in a sus4-"3" suspension, the bass might proceed to another note on the upbeat, subverting the expected third (with the bass) at the moment of resolution. Because of the potential bass movement, syncopes considered weak (because of resolutions to perfect intervals) become more acceptable; e.g., in a sus9-"8," the bass (in second or third species) could proceed to create a 6 in place of the 8 at the upbeat.

Other new three-part sonorities shown by Schenker include a 6 with sus2 and 6 with sus4 (CF in the middle voice). Sonorities such as these occurring on downbeats are mostly incomplete seventh chords and their inversions. Because of movement in the second- and third-species parts, there are too many possibilities for all dissonant suspensions to be evaluated systematically.

The second-species part can either prolong or change the harmony on the upbeat. A change of harmony might resolve a seventh chord created at the downbeat.

Absolutes

1. All standard voice-leading prohibitions, cross relations, and rules of melodic structure remain in force.

2. The second-species part must be consonant with the fourth species on the upbeats. (Since the upbeats prepare the new suspensions and may resolve downbeat dissonances, they must be consonant.)

3. The second-species part may present a passing tone on the upbeat that is dissonant with the CF, but it must still be conso-

nant with the upbeat fourth-species part. It is not easy to get this to work smoothly, because in this combination the second-species part tends to skip frequently. An example cited by Schenker from Bellermann: CF as G4 in middle voice; soprano: fourth-species part with suspension to F♯5 (half note) resolving to E5 (tied); bass: B3 to C♯4 (a dissonant passing tone with the G4 but consonant with the E5). On the following bar the E5 is tied in the soprano, the CF proceeds to F♯4, and the bass resolves the dissonant C♯4 passing tone to D4.

4. (The behavior of the second quarter of the third-species part amidst a dissonant fourth-species suspension is fairly complex; this rule and the next several distill several points treated by Schenker at greater length.) The second quarter of the third-species part must not leap to a dissonant suspended pitch. Because this suspended pitch is dissonant, it must resolve downward by step. When the third-species part follows accordingly, the result is a parallel octave or unison.

5. The second quarter note of the third-species part must not anticipate the resolution tone of the fourth-species part. This follows from the general rule of not anticipating a note resolution.

6. The second or fourth quarter of the third-species part must not leap to a dissonance with the fourth-species part if it creates a new harmony, since the effect is too harsh. For example: soprano (fourth species): C5 (tied to) proceeding to B4; middle (CF): F4; bass (third species): A3 - D4 - E4 - F4. The move from A3 to D4 implies an F major to D minor-seventh harmonic change.

7. There are three admissible instances of the second quarter of the third-species part leaping:

a) The second quarter can restate the pitch of the CF.

b) The second quarter can take a pitch of the triad implied by the resolution of the fourth-species part on the upbeat.

c) The second quarter can add a 5 or 6 interval to what is an incomplete seventh chord tied-to on the downbeat; that is, it might prolong the downbeat harmony.

Preferences and Hints

8. The third quarter of the third-species part may create a dissonant passing tone against the upbeat of the fourth-species part. In this instance, however, the fourth quarter of the third-species line should be consonant with the fourth-species upbeat. In general this effect should be used with care, since the required consonant preparation of the suspension is compromised. An example that works: soprano (fourth species): F5 (tied to) to E5; middle (CF): G4; bass: B3 - C4 - D4 - E4. The clash between the E5 and D4 on the upbeat is mitigated by the E4 on the fourth quarter. Also note here that the implied V7-I of C major is so smooth that the dissonance is absorbed into the progression.

9. Occasional use of dissonant neighboring tones in the third-species part may be permitted in order to work out of difficult situations.

Exercises

Complete three versions of the following CF in three parts. The two ctpts. should be in second and fourth species. Vary the placement of the CF and the species parts in each version and place the second-species part in the bass for one of the settings.

Exercise 14-1: Ab3 - C4 - Db4 - F4 - Eb4 - G4 - Ab4 - Eb4 - C4 - Bb3 - Ab3 (in Ab major)

Complete three versions of the following CF in three parts. The two ctpts. should be in the third and fourth species. Vary the placement of the CF and the species parts in each version and place the third-species part in the bass for one of the settings.

Exercise 14-2: B3 - F♯4 - G4 - E4 - F♯4 - G♯4 - A♯4 - B4 - F♯4 - E4 - C♯4 - B3 (in B minor)

Chapter 15

Combined Species with the Mixed Species; Imitation

[Schenker 2, 251–57]

This setting consists of two lines in the mixed species against the CF. In working with this setting, we begin to approach the sound of free composition. Because of its importance in contrapuntal music of all styles, imitation is introduced in this setting. The combined mixed species also helps serve as a bridge to Part Three, an introduction to free composition modeled on the idealized grammar we have developed for renaissance counterpoint.

Absolutes

1. All standard voice-leading prohibitions, cross relations, and rules of melodic structure remain in force.

2. Materials on the mixed species (chapters 6 and 13) should be reviewed, especially combinations of the species within measures. Some important points:

   a) Whenever the mixed-species lines are in a particular type of species, the rules of that species are in force.

b) In the rhythm of two quarter notes followed by a half note, the half note must be syncopated (tied).

c) Do not tie from the fourth quarter note in a bar.

3. If the mixed-species lines move together in the same note values, they should do so in imperfect consonances (thirds or sixths).

4. This is the key rule in writing two lines together in the mixed species: whenever one mixed-species line presents faster note values against a slower-moving line, conceive of the note values of the slower line as providing a momentary first-species part against which the faster line moves.

5. For our purposes, the two lines in mixed species must imitate each other at the beginning of the exercise. To begin an exercise with imitation:

a) Choose one of the mixed-species parts and begin to write mostly in the second or fourth species: the melodic idea should generally feature long note values. This melody, stated at the beginning in one part before the other enters, is often called a *motivic idea, motive, head motive,* or *motif.* It is also called a *subject,* especially when motivically related to the remainder of the piece.

b) After writing the first two to five notes of the first part, turn to the second mixed-species part and try to find a time interval (usually 2-6 beats after the first part begins) in which the second part can begin with the same motive transposed to another scale step. The transposition of the motive must preserve its *contour* (identical up-and-down interval duplication of the opening part), and still work correctly with the CF. You may have to experiment with various transposition levels to find an imitation that works, although transposition at the fourth and fifth are the most common and should be tried first. Any transposing should be diatonic; i.e., it should not introduce any chromatic pitches. In diatonic transposition, intervals such as seconds or thirds will often change between minor and major.

c) The imitation in the second part is sometimes called the *answer*.

d) If no imitation is possible, revise the first part.

e) Once you find an imitation that works, continue the first part in counterpoint to the second. The beginning of the exercise, with both parts presenting the same motivic idea, is called an *exposition*. Once the exposition is complete, it is often a good strategy to write the cadence, then work backwards to fill in the middle of the exercise.

f) The imitation need only happen at the beginning of the exercise; that is, once the exposition is complete, compose both parts freely.

g) The remainder of the exercise should not recall the opening motivic idea. (Explicit use of the opening motive as a subject is more typical of baroque style.)

Preferences and Hints

6. It is now permissible to write rhythms of a dotted-half note followed by a quarter note in the mixed-species lines.

7. It is also now permissible to write whole notes anywhere in the exercise. They may stand alone, may be tied to a half or whole note in the subsequent bar, or may be tied to a consonant quarter note in the subsequent bar. It is recommended that whole notes be used primarily for imitative beginnings, since they can hinder the flow of an exercise when appearing later.

8. It is useful to focus on exercises in which the middle voice is the CF. Once an exercise is complete, the CF can be removed so that the mixed-species lines function alone as a two-voice framework (if we allow for the large range between the voices). This two-voice framework itself approximates a free renaissance composition in two parts.

9. An imitation may be as few as two notes. It is recommended, however, that imitative subjects be at least three notes; four to six notes is ideal.

Exercises

For each CF, write three exercises in three parts with two lines in the mixed species. Begin each version with imitation in the mixed-species parts. For each version, the CF should be in a different part.

Continue to label the intervals and check, as usual, to be sure no forbidden motions occur.

From now on, write all exercises in 4/2 time rather than 2/2. This means that there will be two CF whole notes per bar. The purpose of the larger-value time signature is to suggest a more flowing, broadly linear style, but the rules remain the same as writing in 2/2. For example, every third beat in 4/2 should be thought of as if it were a downbeat in a 2/2 bar.

A helpful way to begin working in 4/2 is to write normally in 2/2, then erase every other barline. Alternatively, write in 4/2, then afterwards add the 2/2 barlines lightly (or in dotted lines) to check that none of the rules have been broken inadvertently.

Exercise 15-1: The Fux D-minor CF: D4 - F4 - E4 - D4 - G4 - F4 - A4 - G4 - F4 - E4- D4

Exercise 15-2: C4 - A♭4 - G4 - E♭4 - F4 - G4 - A♮4 - B♮4 - C5 - G4 - E♭4 - D4 - C4 (in C minor)

Part Three

Free Composition

Chapter 16

Modulation (Cadences to New Key Centers)

Part Three of this text explores the basics of two-part free composition in the idealized (and simplified) renaissance style developed in Parts One and Two. The most important principles to be introduced are 1) writing without cantus firmus, 2) writing imitative expositions (as described in chapter 15), and 3) cadencing to scale degrees other than the tonic.

We introduce cadencing to non-tonic scale degrees in order to extend the length of the exercises and approximate more closely the composing of real music. Cadencing to non-tonic scale degrees usually introduces chromatic pitches—particularly leading tones—to heighten the sense of arrival on these secondary scale steps. Although such cadences are generally brief, we will informally call any cadences to scale steps other than the tonic *modulations*.

Interestingly, exercises in the minor mode will often project a significant but non-primary tonal center. When such exercises use the descending melodic minor scale, which has the same pitches as its relative major, they can sound as if they were momentarily in the relative major key. In the Fux D minor CF (Exercise 2-1), for example, the fifth and sixth notes, G and F, are often harmonized by an implied V-I progression in F major, the relative major of D minor. More generally, the treatment of the

relative major in the minor mode embodies the basic principle of
cadencing to other key centers.

Absolutes

1. For exercises in free composition, we shall allow non-tonic
cadences to the following scale degrees:

   a) In the major mode—
   iii (minor); IV (major); V (major); vi (minor)

   b) In the minor mode—
   III (major); v (minor); VI (major); ♭VII (major)

Although we are writing in two parts without the possibility of
complete triads, we follow the convention of using uppercase
Roman numerals for major chords and lowercase Roman numerals for minor chords, since there is the implication of a momentary key center associated with each of these scale degrees.

2. As discussed in chapter 1, any direct chromatic movement
must be avoided within a melodic line. For example, in a modulation from C major to G major, F♮ may not proceed directly to F♯
since this is an explicit chromaticism, a dissonant melodic succession of an augmented unison. (Compare the avoidance of successions of ↓6̂ and ↑6̂ or ↓7̂ and ↑7̂ in the minor mode.)

3. Notes that will be chromatically altered should be *neutralized*
by motion to, usually, a member of the tonic triad (or some lo-
cally more stable pitch). In the preceding example given in rule
#2, F♮ should proceed (ideally) to E, *then* to F♯.

4. After a cadence to a new tonal center, return to the original
tonic is effected by *neutralization*, then *cancellation* of the
chromatic tones. To continue the previous example (from rules

#2 and #3), the F♯ (in G major) should be neutralized by motion to G, then canceled by F♮ in returning to C major.

5. In most cases, cancellation of chromatic tones should take place in the same register as the chromatic tone. If not, the juxtaposition of different chromatic versions of the same pitch in different registers may be too harsh, i.e., cause a *cross relation*. If the cancellation of the chromatic pitch must occur in another register, it is important 1) that the first pitch be neutralized in the proper register and 2) that there be sufficient temporal distance between it and the second (canceled) version of the pitch. (Cross relations can occur within single melodic lines but most often occur between lines.) Sometimes neutralization and cancellation will take place in another part.

Exercises

Exercise 16-1a: In the key of E♭ major, write four first-species CFs. Each melody should modulate to and cadence on one of the permissible tonal centers (iii, IV, V, and vi) before returning to the tonic. The melodies should begin and end on the tonic pitch and be ten to sixteen bars long in 4/2 time (two whole notes per bar and ending with a double whole note).

Exercise 16-1b: In the key of F♯ minor, write four first-species CFs. Each melody should modulate to and cadence on one of the permissible tonal centers (III, v, VI, and ♭VII) before returning to the tonic. The melodies should begin and end on the tonic pitch and be ten to sixteen bars long in 4/2 time (two whole notes per bar and ending with a double whole note).

Exercise 16-2: From the CFs created in Exercise 16-1a, select the one that cadenced on V.

a) Let the CF serve as a middle voice for a three-part exercise in the combined mixed species.

b) The two parts in the mixed species should begin with imitation (as described in chapter 15).

c) Take care that the modulations to and from the new key center are handled correctly, with accidentals properly neutralized and canceled.

d) Continue to write in 4/2 time.

e) Be sure the two-voice framework works well without the CF.

Chapter 17

Two-Part Free Counterpoint to the First Cadence

In the preceding two chapters, we investigated 1) imitating the entrances of different lines and 2) cadencing to scale degrees other than the tonic before returning to the principal tonality. We are now ready to construct two-part ctpts. whose entrances are in imitation and unsupported by a CF.

Absolutes

1. Continue to write in 4/2 time. (Assume that 4/2 time will be customary from now on.) It is now possible to repeat half notes, whole notes, and double whole notes in the melodies.

2. At each moment in the exercise, any two parts in contrapuntal relationship either have the same or different note values. Each case in turn:

> a) If the note values of the two parts are the same, the passage should follow the rules of the two-part first species. That is, the voices should move together in consonances, with particular emphasis on thirds and sixths. Perfect intervals should be used more rarely and must not be approached

by similar motion. Parallel perfect consonances must be
avoided.

b) If the note values are different, then the slower note provides a momentary CF for the other voice. Accordingly,
write the voice with the faster note values in the two-part
mixed species relative to the slower note.

3. Continue to write for adjacent voices (soprano-alto, alto-tenor,
or tenor-bass), as described in chapter 2. The exercise must begin
with a single voice stating an opening motive. As stated previously, the opening motive should stress longer note values, i.e.,
double whole, whole, and half notes; quarter notes should occur
less often, eighth notes almost never. The three-beat value of a
whole note tied to a half note may also be used as part of the
subject.

4. The second voice enters in imitation to the first. (Review
chapter 15 for specifics on imitation.)

5. Once the exposition of the opening motive is complete, assume that the music continues for two to four 4/2 bars until the
first cadence. Write in barlines to show the empty bars that lead
to this first cadence.

6. Write the cadence to the new key. Use the following steps:

a) Choose either the upper or the lower part.

b) Write a fourth-species cadence for the chosen part in the
following manner: tie the chosen interior scale step as a half
note to itself on the fourth beat, or write it as a whole note on
the second beat. This will syncopate the chosen scale step.

c) Follow the interior scale step with its *own* leading tone as
a half note.

d) Complete the cadence by returning to interior scale step as a double whole note.

e) Take the second voice and write a ctpt. that supports the cadence. For example, the second voice could (in the new key) proceed $\hat{3}$-$\hat{2}$-$\hat{1}$ as whole notes. (Important note: these scale steps apply to the new key.) If we assume that the first voice was the upper part, the $\hat{3}$-$\hat{2}$-$\hat{1}$ in the lower part will enable the $\hat{1}$ in the upper part to be prepared as a consonance (over $\hat{3}$). When the lower part proceeds to $\hat{2}$, the upper part will have a sus7 (suspension) over the $\hat{2}$, which must resolve to the leading-tone $\hat{7}$ (as a sixth over the lower $\hat{2}$). Finally, both parts resolve by expanding to an octave $\hat{1}$ of the new key. The tonality of the new key is established and the cadence is complete.

f) It is also possible to use a decorated cadence for the part in the fourth species. (For decorated cadences, review earlier material on the mixed species.)

7. Once the cadence to the new key is complete, return to and complete the music that connects the end of the exposition to the new cadence.

Preferences and Hints

8. A temporary CF can be used as a middle (third) voice if desired. Such a CF may help reduce "blank page" anxiety. Further, since the CF is arbitrary, it can be changed whenever necessary. However, because the two fifth-species parts must sound well without it, they must not use too many perfect intervals or proceed in similar motion to perfect intervals. Note that a temporary CF as a middle voice often creates too large a span between the outer parts when they are listened to independently, a drawback to using this technique.

9. While writing the imitations that cadence to the various scale steps, bear in mind the treatment of the accidentals involved: the original tonality should be anchored. This is often accomplished by stating or implying a tonic triad of the original tonality at the outset. Scale steps that will be altered when cadencing to the following interior scale step should be used, if possible, to establish the initial tonality still more firmly.

10. The transition to the new scale step can be made smoother if a measure or two is included that features the in-common tones between the two keys. These common tones provide what are called (more generally) *pivot* chords or harmonies.

11. In general, scale steps that define very close key areas, such as V in the major mode or III in the minor, will occur more often than distant scale steps.

Exercises

As described in rule #8, a temporary CF can be used as a middle (third) voice for the following exercises. The exercises must work well without it, however.

Exercise 17-1 (a, b, c, d): Take a single opening motive in the major mode and practice devising two-part imitations that cadence, in turn, to all the permissible scale steps: iii, IV, V, and vi. That is, after composing a single beginning that establishes a tonic, write four continuations that proceed to each of the scale steps in turn. It is not necessary to cadence back to the tonic.

Exercise 17-2 (a, b, c, d): As in exercise 17-1, take a single opening motive in the minor mode and practice devising two-part imitations that cadence, in turn, to all the permissible scale steps: III, v, VI, and ♭VII.

Chapter 18

More on Imitation; First Piece

In addition to direct imitation, there are three other imitative techniques that will be discussed in this chapter. We shall also examine how the exercise should be continued after cadencing to a new scale step, and, in so doing, outline a method for composing a short two-part composition.

Absolutes

1. In addition to standard imitation, certain variants of imitation technique are very common in contrapuntal writing. Recall that the first part is sometimes called the "subject" and the second part (in imitation) called the "answer."

a) The answer can *invert* the subject. Each interval in the subject that rises or descends is answered by the opposite rising or descending interval in the answer. The inversions tend to remain diatonic. Hence, in the key of C, if the subject proceeds C4-E4, the inverted answer might proceed C4-A3 or (transposed) G3-E3. (Inversions can take place at various intervals, like standard answers.) Because the key is C major, the thirds take the notes of the C major scale; i.e., the rising (major) third from C is answered by the descending (minor) third from C.

b) The answer can halve the note values of the subject, a technique called *diminution*. For example, if the subject is stated in half notes, the answer enters with the same motive, possibly transposed at some interval, in quarter notes.

c) The answer can double the note values of the subject, a technique called *augmentation*. For example, if the subject is stated in quarter notes, the answer enters with the same motive, possibly transposed at some interval, in half notes.

d) *Double diminution* and *double augmentation,* involving quadruple temporal relationships, are also possible.

e) The preceding forms can be combined; hence, it is possible to invert a subject while doubling its note values, i.e., *inverted diminution.*

2. To continue after the exercise cadences to another key:

a) Only the part proceeding from the leading tone of the new key to its tonic will cadence completely: as usual, proceed from $\hat{7}$ to $\hat{1}$.

b) Instead of resolving the other part from $\hat{2}$ or $\hat{5}$ to $\hat{1}$, substitute a half or quarter rest for the $\hat{1}$.

c) After the rest in the second part, begin a new melodic entrance while the first part is holding $\hat{1}$. It is often desirable to begin the new melodic entrance with the expected note that was omitted.

d) The second part initiates a *new* melodic motive. The first part, after establishing the new tonic, may rest during the presentation of the new melodic motive.

e) The first part then enters in imitation of the second. Various techniques described in rule #1 may be applied.

3. Choose a new scale step to cadence to. The music should continue about three to six bars before the new scale step is reached. At this point, write the next cadence. However, alternate the roles of the voices for the new cadence: whichever part supported the fourth-species cadence in rule #1 now should itself provide the syncopation. The alternate part will then provide the support.

Exercises

Exercise 18-1 (a, b, c): Using the techniques described in rule #1, write three two-part imitations that begin in one key and cadence, after two to five 4/2 bars, on a new scale step. In each of the exercises, practice one of the following: inversion, augmentation, and diminution. Two of the exercises should be in the minor mode, the other in the major. For permissible scale steps in modulating (for both the major and minor modes), review chapter 16, rule #1.

Exercise 18-2 (Short Two-Voice Piece): Your first piece will consist of two short sections, each beginning with imitation and closing to a cadence. Each phrase should be three to eight 4/2 bars. The first phrase should close on some scale step other than the tonic; V is best for the major mode and III for the minor. The second phrase should continue the exercise according to rules #2 through #5 above and return to close on the tonic.

The imitation beginning the second phrase will be of a different subject.

Although the two subjects in your piece are distinct, the two sections must have a similar character in order to create a unified composition.

Experiment with including inversion, augmentation, or diminution in your piece.

Chapter 19

Invertible Counterpoint (Octave)

Polyphonic compositions are sometimes written with the plan that pairs of lines will be inverted registrally. This means that the two lines in question exchange roles as treble and bass, a technique called *invertible counterpoint* or *double counterpoint*. A useful consequence is that a passage of successfully written music may be conveniently transformed into another that also works successfully: one gets "music for free."

Two lines are inverted *at the octave* when one line remains constant while the other is transposed up or down one or more octaves until their registral order is reversed.

Another way of achieving the same result is to transpose the treble down a certain (diatonic) interval and the bass up another certain interval, such that these two intervals add up to nine.

Absolutes

1. For two lines to invert correctly (at any interval), it is necessary that no impermissible dissonances result. The following shows the diatonic intervals and their inversions at the octave:

Diatonic interval:	1 2 3 *4 5* 6 7 8
Octave inversion:	8 7 6 *5 4* 3 2 1

The fifth, which (unless diminished) is always consonant, inverts to the fourth, which in two parts is always dissonant. Otherwise, all the consonant intervals remain consonant and all the dissonant intervals remain dissonant. Hence, for two lines to invert successfully at the octave, they must not treat the fifth as a consonance. Except for this one caveat, two lines may generally be inverted at the octave without problematic consequence.

While lines must not treat the fifth as a consonance in order to invert at the octave, fifths can certainly be used as passing tones. When inverted, they will be treated correctly as passing (dissonant) fourths.

When a passage is repeated, but in invertible counterpoint, a *repeated block* occurs. That is, the original two-part texture forms a block, or passage, of music that is then repeated after the operation of invertible counterpoint. Repeated blocks can occur with other operations as well, the most common being transposition.

Preferences and Hints

2. Suspensions also invert successfully at the octave. For example, by comparing the intervals in the preceding diagram, you will note that a sus7-6 suspension inverts to a sus2-3 and vice versa. In general, for invertible ctpt. at the octave, the "good" suspensions invert to good ones, the "bad" ones to bad.

3. Lines that work together in ctpt. can also be transposed diatonically as a unit. When one transposes each line in the same direction at the same interval, the resulting music has the same melodic layout as the original but new harmonic implications. (A pair of lines can also be transposed chromatically, but that operation merely changes the key while preserving the harmonic relationships.) Such an operation can be applied to invertible counterpoint as well. For example, assume that two lines work well in ctpt. and do not treat the fifth as a consonance. While

they will invert at the octave, the resulting music might not be varied enough to be interesting. However, if the inverted pair of lines is also transposed diatonically, the effect of the transposition in addition to the interchange of upper and lower parts may together yield useful results.

Exercise

Exercise 19-1 (Second Piece): Write a two-part piece in three phrases with two interior cadences. The first interior cadence may be to 1̂ or another scale degree; the second interior cadence must be to a scale degree other than 1̂. The last phrase should cadence back to 1̂. Imitation must occur at the beginning and after the two interior cadences. Other imitative moments can be incorporated as well. Invertible ctpt. at the octave must also occur in the piece. Label the corresponding passages in invertible ctpt. You may also wish to incorporate imitative inversion, augmentation, or diminution.

Chapter 20

More on Invertible Counterpoint

Invertible (or double) ctpt. at the octave does not alter the tonal significance of the two parts (unless they are diatonically transposed or pitches are chromatically altered). Invertible ctpt. at the twelfth is richer in possibilities because the tonal implications of the lines change.

Of the various possible (diatonic) intervals of inversion, double ctpt. at the tenth is the third type in more or less common use. It is more unwieldy than inversion at the octave or twelfth, as will be made clear.

Mirroring is another contrapuntal technique that is occasionally seen; it is described briefly.

Absolutes

1. Two lines are inverted at the twelfth when one line remains constant while the other is transposed up or down a twelfth until their bass and treble roles are exchanged. Other ways of inverting lines at the twelfth are:

a) The upper part may be transposed a fifth down, while the lower part is transposed an octave up.

b) The lower part may be transposed a fifth up, while the upper part is transposed an octave down.

c) Other combinations of inversions may be used—the lower part transposing up a certain interval, the upper part down a certain interval—but these two intervals must add to 13.

The following shows the diatonic intervals and their resulting inversions at the twelfth:

Diatonic Interval: 1 2   3 4 5 *6* *7* 8 9 10 11 12
Twelfth Inversion: 12 11 10 9 8 *7* *6* 5 4 3   2   1

2. Some consequences of inversion at the twelfth:

a) The avoidance of parallel perfect consonances remains unaffected. (Compare double ctpt. at the tenth below.) For example, potential parallel fifths in the original become potential parallel octaves under the operation.

b) The sixth cannot be used as a consonance in the original ctpt., since it becomes a seventh under the operation.

c) As a result of (b), the sus7-6 suspension cannot be used.

d) Thus, sevenths and sixths should be passing tones. Under inversion, their function as consonances or dissonances reverses.

e) The sus2-3 and sus4-3 suspensions invert to the other.

3. Two lines are inverted at the tenth when one line remains constant while the other is transposed up or down a tenth until their registral order is changed. Other ways of inverting lines at the tenth are:

a) The upper part may be transposed a third down, while the lower part is transposed an octave up.

b) The lower part may be transposed a third up, while the upper part is transposed an octave down.

c) Other combinations of inversions may be used—the lower transposing up a certain interval, the upper down a certain interval—but these two intervals must add to 11.

The following shows the diatonic intervals and their inversions at the tenth:

Diatonic Interval: 1 2 *3* 4 *5* *6* 7 *8* 9 10
Tenth Inversion: 10 9 *8* 7 *6* *5* 4 *3* 2 1

4. Some consequences of inversion at the tenth:

a) Consonances and dissonances remain unchanged under inversion.

b) Perfect and imperfect consonances reverse. Hence, any parallel motion between imperfect consonances must be avoided, because under inversion this becomes a parallelism between perfect consonances.

c) Hence, for the lines to invert successfully, all consonances must proceed in contrary motion.

d) Suspensions should be handled with care or avoided. For example, the sus7-6 inverts to a much less good sus4-5; the sus4-3 becomes a sus7-8, which is always weak.

5. A *mirror inversion* of a block occurs when the parts are interchanged and the melodic motions of each part inverted. An interesting consequence of this technique is that the vertical intervals remain unchanged. As with invertible ctpt., mirror inversions can be placed at a variety of transpositions.

Preferences and Hints

6. It is often productive to operate on a block through invertible ctpt., mirroring, or transposition, and then add appropriate accidentals afterwards in order to smooth out the lines' harmonic implications.

7. When a passage is to be inverted at the tenth, it is useful to include sufficient perfect consonances so as to obtain sufficient imperfect consonances after inversion.

Exercises

Exercise 20-1 (a, b): Write two passages of two-part ctpt. approximately three 4/2 bars in length that can be inverted a) at the twelfth and b) at the tenth. Bracket the blocks and label to show their relationship.

Exercise 20-2 (Third Piece): Write a four-phrase composition in two-part ctpt. that modulates and cadences to three interior scale steps, two of them other than the tonic. The piece should return to the tonic for the ending. Use imitative entries at the beginning and after each cadence. Try to incorporate imitative inversion, augmentation, or diminution. You must incorporate a passage that later appears in invertible ctpt. at either the tenth or twelfth. Label both the original passage and its appearance in invertible ctpt.

Appendices

Appendix 1

Four-Part First Species

[Schenker 2, 124–45]

The four-part first-species setting consists of three first-species lines against the CF. Despite the availability of four-note chords, the seventh chord may not be used in this setting. This is because the first species permits no dissonances, and the interval of a seventh (or, inverted, a second) renders any seventh chord dissonant.

Because complete triads must have a pitch doubled in four-part writing, the first species is helpful in examining the general nature of doubling. Two separate doublings or even triplings become necessary with incomplete triads; these are permissible.

Whereas in three-part writing there is a variety of possible voice combinations, in four-part writing the standard soprano, alto, tenor, bass (SATB) choir is the customary medium. Write with a four-staff system, and use alto clef for the alto part and tenor clef for the tenor part to practice these clefs.

Absolutes

1. All standard voice-leading prohibitions, cross relations, and rules of melodic structure remain in force.

2. In doublings of perfect consonances of complete triads, the best is the octave above the bass; the next best are the bass itself (unison) or the fifth above the bass.

3. In doublings of imperfect consonances of complete triads, the third is preferred over the sixth.

4. For incomplete triads, doubling the perfect consonances sounds too empty, hence the imperfect consonances (third and sixth) must be doubled. Avoid open fifths or octaves; instead, include a third or sixth from the root and double this pitch. For example, C3-E3-E4-C5 or C3-A3-A4-C5 are possible, but not C3-G3-G4-C5 or C3-C4-C4-C5.

5. Similar motion to perfect consonances is less problematic than in three-part writing, because the voice leading of the individual parts recedes into the thicker texture. Hence, similar motion to perfect fifths and octaves is generally permissible, especially when:

a) at least one of the four voices moves by a second, preferably the highest

b) the second chord of the pair is a complete triad

c) the third and/or fourth voice proceed(s) in contrary motion

The extent to which the above conditions are satisfied increases the likelihood that the progression will be successful. Deviations from these rules are more apparent in the upper voices than in the lower.

6. Avoid extended successions of thirds in the lower two voices.

7. When the CF is in the soprano, alto, or tenor, the bass must cadence with $\hat{5}$-$\hat{1}$. As a result of this motion, the final chord will contain a tripled tonic and the third. This third could be replaced by the fifth for a more archaic cadence.

8. When the bass cadences from $\hat{2}$ to $\hat{1}$ (i.e., the CF is in the bass), the best penultimate sonority is the vii° 6-3 chord with the third over the bass (i.e., the $\hat{4}$) doubled. The $\hat{4}$s proceed in contrary motion to the fifth and third of the final tonic chord. The penultimate 6-3 chord could also double the $\hat{2}$, though motion to the final chord will be less smooth.

Preferences and Hints

9. As always, the outer voices should define a two-part framework that works well by itself.

10. A root-position tonic triad (complete or incomplete) is preferred in the first bar.

11. The bass can acquire a more harmonic role; hence, it may skip more freely than the other parts.

12. Voice crossings are permissible. Even nonadjacent voices can be crossed if circumstances require it.

13. The overtone series provides a basis for voicing all sonorities (both complete and incomplete triads) with the larger intervals below the smaller. Other voicings are certainly possible, but this arrangement is generally considered the "most natural."

Exercise

Select a CF from the preceding chapters. Do two or three settings with the CF in different voices.

Exercise Ap1-1: A four-part setting in the first species.

Appendix 2

Four-Part Simple Species
(Second, Third, Fourth, Mixed)

[Schenker 2, 146–67]

Recall that "simple species" is defined by use of the first species in all parts except the one named by the species. In general, for the second, third, fourth, and mixed simple species, the principles remain the same as in three-part simple species.

Absolutes

1. All standard voice-leading prohibitions, cross relations, and rules of melodic structure remain in force.

2. The rules of triad completeness and incompleteness are the same as in the four-part first-species setting (appendix 1). Many of these derive from the three-part first species, except for issues involving the doubling of pitches.

3. As in the two- and three-part second species, dissonant neighbor notes must be avoided.

4. Avoid a 6-4 (second-inversion) triad at the beginning of the exercise, even if the entering line in the bass (when it has the second-, third-, or fourth-species part) adds the root to the chord to create a root-position triad.

5. In the fourth species, syncopes in either of the upper three parts are conceived and named in relation to the bass. Syncopes in the bass are conceived and named in relation to all three upper parts.

6. As in the three-part fourth species, avoid doubling the tone of resolution, unless you are filling out a weaker suspension.

7. As in the two- and three-part fourth species, a dissonant syncope must descend by step to its resolution.

8. It is often desirable to plan a V chord supporting an 8-7 passing motion at the cadence. This configuration results in a V7 chord on the upbeat of the penultimate bar, the dissonant passing seventh resolving to the $\hat{3}$ of the I chord in the final bar.

Preferences and Hints

9. A unison between two parts may be used more frequently in four-part writing than in two- or three-part writing, because the thicker texture helps cover any emptiness.

10. Fux will sometimes introduce a second-species half note into a first-species part if the voice leading of the syncopated voice requires it. Schenker generally disapproves of this process, preferring to reserve it for the combined species (simultaneous use of different species in different voices).

Exercise

For the following CF, write four four-part simple-species exercises. Do the first exercise with the second species, the second exercise with the third species, the third exercise with the fourth species, and the fourth exercise with the mixed species. In each version, place the simple-species part and the CF in a different voice.

Exercise Ap2-1 (a, b, c, d): C4 - G4 - E♭4 - A♭4 - G4 - B♮4 - C5 - G4 - F4 - D4 - C4 (in C minor)

Appendix 3

Five-, Six-, Seven-, and Eight-Part Counterpoint

[Schenker 2, 168–74]

These exercises consist of a CF and multiple first-species lines supporting a single line in the first-, second-, third-, fourth-, or mixed-species setting.

Absolutes

1. All standard voice-leading prohibitions, cross relations, and rules of melodic structure remain in force, although the strictness of these rules can be relaxed somewhat because of the thicker texture.

2. No new principles are introduced. Refer to previous rules for each of the species types.

3. While most doublings are acceptable, and indeed less problematic than in three- or four-part ctpt., the leading tone must not be doubled.

Preferences and Hints

4. It is acceptable to cross voices more often than in three- and four-part ctpt.

5. With the thickness of texture, similar motion to perfect consonances becomes less obvious than in three- and four-part ctpt. and hence easier to handle.

Exercise

Select a species (probably the second species is best) and set the following CF in six voices. Put the species line in one of the middle voices.

Exercise Ap3-1: F#4 - C#5 - A4 - D5 - C#5 - D#5 - E#5 - F#5 - B4 - C#5 - A4 - G#4 - F#4 (in F# minor)

Appendix 4

Four-Part Combined Counterpoints

[Schenker 2, 200–3, 207–9]

For four-part writing that combines the second and third species, the combinations are a) one first species, one second species, and one third species, b) two second species and one third species, c) two third species and one first species, d) two third species and one second species, and e) three third species. Combinations with the fourth species are treated below. The following rules mostly recall procedures associated with the combined second and third species (chapter 11).

Absolutes

1. In settings with two second-species lines, such lines should avoid excessive parallel thirds and sixths.

2. In settings with two second-species lines, such lines must remain consonant with each other.

3. In the less strict setting with the second and third species, the third quarter note may be dissonant with the upbeat half notes.

4. In settings with three third-species lines, chains of 6-3 and 6-4 chords are possible. As internal dissonances within the three third-species lines, the 6-4 chords must pass to a consonance. Otherwise, the three third-species lines must remain consonant with each other, even when all three are dissonant to the CF.

* * *

[Schenker 2, 226–28, 242–49]

For four-part writing incorporating the fourth species, the combinations are f) one first species, one second species, and one fourth species, g) two second species and one fourth species, h) one first species, one third species, and one fourth species, i) one second species, one third species, and one fourth species, and j) two third species and one fourth species.

In comparison to three-voice combinations that include the fourth species, there are in general no new problems associated with four-voice writing. Schenker does point out, however, that its addition allows complete seventh chords, for example, the 6 with sus5 and 3 on the downbeat in setting (i). Material from chapter 14 (three-part writing with the syncopated species) should be reviewed.

Exercise

Exercise Ap4-1: Select a CF from the previous chapters and write an exercise with one part in each species, i.e., combination (i).

Appendix 5

Three- or Four-Part Kyrie; Stretto

A study of effective free composition for voices would take us beyond the scope of this book, for such a topic is part of the study of composition proper (or the study of orchestration), and this text's purpose, rather, is to develop compositional exercises in abstract counterpoint based on an idealized renaissance model. In the study of composition proper, such issues as setting text would be considered in detail. However, this appendix is included to provide an opportunity to marshal the contrapuntal skills you have developed into composing a standard Kyrie (from the Catholic mass) in three or four voices.

If you have practiced working in four or more voices (see the previous appendices), try writing for four voices. Otherwise, write for three.

If your free contrapuntal writing to this point has been in two and three parts only, then use this opportunity to write freely for three parts. There is essentially no new material in writing three (or more) parts freely that has not been discussed in the chapters on three-part species.

Absolutes; Stretto

1. Because your Kyrie is written to be sung, be sure to observe the standard vocal ranges. If you write for three voices, you

should decide, in particular, whether your middle voice is to be an alto or tenor.

2. An advantage to writing for four voices is the opportunity to vary the texture. Palestrina and the other great sixteenth-century composers took advantage of the number of textures possible with four (and more) voices by often combining two or three parts at a time. This practice allows unusual combinations of voices, such as a high sopranos and altos with the bass in a wholly different register. Further, the parts can then rest individually for several bars from time to time.

3. You may wish to incorporate the use of *stretto*, another contrapuntal device. Stretto is defined as a second part entering in imitation to a first part before the first part has finished its statement of the subject. In other words, the imitative subjects *overlap*. It works most effectively as a climax for three or more voices, since the overlapping generates momentum and cumulative excitement.

4. The time interval of the imitation in creating a stretto may be chosen freely, but if it takes too long for the later parts to enter, the stretto will be less effective.

5. The imitation in stretto:

    a) may occur at any transposed interval that works
    b) invert the subject
    c) present it in augmentation or diminution

6. Stretto also works best at climactic moments late in a piece, because the listener has heard the subject several times and can separate its entrances aurally despite their overlapping.

7. Stretto cannot be freely applied to any subject because its structure may not permit the overlap without introducing impermissible dissonances. Instead, you must write your subject with its eventual stretto planned in advance. A simple example would

be this subject in half notes: C3-D3-E3-C3-A3-G3-E3. It can be answered in stretto (at the half note) by the following (beginning at the first part's second half note, the D3): F4-G4-A4-F4-D5-C5. Note that the answering statement is transposed up an eleventh and that the time interval is a half note.

Exercise

Exercise Ap5-1: Compose an ABA Kyrie in three or four voices.

The text for the Kyrie is:

• First A Section: "Kyrie Eleison, Kyrie Eleison, Kyrie Eleison."

• B Section: "Christe Eleison, Christe Eleison, Christe Eleison."

• Second A Section: "Kyrie Eleison, Kyrie Eleison, Kyrie Eleison."

Within each section you may repeat the phrases as often as you like, but traditionally each phrase is intoned three times. For examples, compare masses by any fine late sixteenth-century composer, such as Palestrina or Lassus.

The phrases must be set *melismatically*. That is, the syllables of the text are held through several of the notes of the phrases and only change at appropriate moments. (In a *syllabic* setting, there is one note per syllable of text.)

Since you are writing parts to be sung, be sure you consider breathing as part of each melodic line. A simple strategy is to try and include rests in one part while another is moving. Be sure to sing each part to be sure it can be sung without difficulty.

The B section should be written in the dominant of whatever key you choose for the A section. Within each section, there should be one or two cadences on scale steps other than the tonic of that section.

Use a variety of textures in distributing the three or four parts among two or three voices at a time. At times, pair off the voices in thirds. If you write in four parts, reserve the use of the tutti for climactic moments.

Begin each phrase with imitation. The subjects beginning each phrase should vary, but there should still be a feeling of continuity.

The B section of the Kyrie should contrast the A section. The two A sections should be similar in feeling but not identical.

You may wish to incorporate homophonic (chordal) textures as a contrast to the imitative sections. These passages, written in the first species, should occur at moments where they create an effective foil to the more flowing counterpoint. An example might be the beginning of the B section.

You should try to build to a strategically placed climax that incorporates the use of stretto. This might occur two-thirds of the way through the second A section. That is, your final statement of the "Kyrie" subject might take one of the preceding imitative entries and treat it in stretto.

Bibliography

The following are studies that deal with renaissance style or apply species counterpoint to the analysis of free composition. The literature of counterpoint is vast and includes many studies devoted to the baroque and the ramifications of the style of J.S. Bach. With the exception of the Benjamin, works treating the counterpoint of that era are not included here.

Benjamin, Thomas. 1986. *Counterpoint in the Style of J. S. Bach.* New York: Schirmer Books.

Dubiel, Joseph. 1990. "'When You Are a Beethoven': Kinds of Rules in Schenker's *Counterpoint.*" *Journal of Music Theory* 34/2: 291–340.

Fux, Johann Joseph. 1725. *Gradus ad Parnassum* [*Steps to Parnassus*]. Available as *The Study of Counterpoint.* Trans. and ed. Alfred Mann. New York: W.W. Norton, 1965.

Gauldin, Robert. 1985. *A Practical Approach to 16th-Century Counterpoint.* Englewood Cliffs, NJ: Prentice-Hall.

Jeppesen, Knud. 1939. *Counterpoint: The Polyphonic Vocal Style of the Sixteenth Century.* Trans. Glen Haydon. New York: Prentice-Hall.

————. 1946. *The Style of Palestrina and the Dissonance.* New York: Oxford University Press. (Reprint, Dover Publications, 1970.)

Lester, Joel. 1989. *Between Modes and Keys: German Theory 1592–1802.* (Harmonologia Series No. 3). Stuyvesant, NY: Pendragon Press.

Mann, Alfred. 1965. *The Study of Counterpoint. See* Fux 1725.

Owen, Harold. 1992. *Modal and Tonal Counterpoint: From Josquin to Stravinsky.* New York: Schirmer Books.

Salzer, Felix, and Carl Schachter. 1969. *Counterpoint in Composition.* New York: McGraw-Hill.

Schenker, Heinrich. 1910, 1922. *Counterpoint: A Translation of Kontrapunkt by Heinrich Schenker* (Volume II of New Musical Theories and Fantasies). 2 vols., trans. John Rothgeb and Jürgen Thym; ed. Rothgeb. New York: Schirmer Books, 1987.

Schoenberg, Arnold. 1963. *Preliminary Exercises in Counterpoint.* London and Boston: Faber and Faber.

Schubert, Peter. 1995. "A Lesson from Lassus: Form in the Duos of 1577." *Music Theory Spectrum* 17/1: 1–26.

Soderlund, Gustave. 1947. *Direct Approach to Counterpoint in Sixteenth-Century Style.* New York: Prentice-Hall.

Soderlund, Gustave Fredric, and Samuel H. Scott. 1971. *Examples of Gregorian Chant and Other Sacred Music of the 16th Century.* Englewood Cliffs, NJ: Prentice-Hall.

Swindale, Owen. 1962. *Polyphonic Composition: An Introduction to the Art of Composing Vocal Counterpoint in the Sixteenth-Century Style.* New York: Oxford University Press.

Thakar, Markand. 1990. *Counterpoint: Fundamentals of Music Making.* New Haven and London: Yale University Press.

Westergaard, Peter. 1975. *An Introduction to Tonal Theory.* New York: W.W. Norton.

Zarlino, Gioseffo. 1558. *The Art of Counterpoint* (Part Three of *Le Istitutioni harmoniche*). Trans. Guy A. Marco and Claude V. Palisca. New York: W.W. Norton, 1976.

Index

About the Author

Henry Martin is professor of music at Rutgers University in Newark. His teachers have included Milton Babbitt and David Del Tredici. With a Ph.D. from Princeton University and degrees from the University of Michigan and Oberlin Conservatory, he has pursued a dual career as a composer-pianist and as a music theorist specializing in jazz and the Western tonal tradition.

Martin's *Preludes and Fugues* won the Barlow Endowment Competition for 1998 and the National Composers Competition sponsored by the League of Composers—International Society for Contemporary Music in 1991. The first half of *Preludes and Fugues* was issued on GM Recordings CD2049 with Sara Davis Buechner as pianist. Bridge Records released the second half of *Preludes and Fugues* with Martin as pianist in 2004 (Bridge 9140).

As a theorist, Martin has published extensively. His books include *Charlie Parker and Thematic Improvisation* (Scarecrow Press, 1996) and a jazz history text, co-written with Keith Waters, *Jazz, the First 100 Years* (Wadsworth-Schirmer, 2002). His articles and reviews have appeared in such journals as *In Theory Only*, *Perspectives of New Music*, *Music & Letters*, and *Music Theory Spectrum*. He is a co-editor of the *Annual Review of Jazz Studies*, which is published by the Institute of Jazz Studies at Rutgers-Newark.

127